ARIES
GARDA
Reds
Esat
Digifone

JIM RYAN

A SPORTING BEAT

The Story of

a Sports-Mad Garda

on STREAM

ONSTREAM PUBLICATIONS
Currabaha, Cloghroe, Co. Cork, Ireland
www.onstream.ie

1 89768 569 6

978 1 89768 569 3

10 9 8 7 6 5 4 3 2 1

The following photographs are reproduced by kind permission: front cover and pages 1, 75 (left), 89, 150, 175, 211 (*Irish Examiner)*; page 24 (John Connery); page 91 (Tony O'Connell); page 93 (Department of Justice); page 207 (SMA).

Printed in England by CPD

Contents

Foreword

There is a book in all of us, so they say, and my book started out from people telling me that I should write down the stories I had told them. A very wise old man in Watergrasshill used to say, 'If you tell a fool to do something often enough, he'll eventually believe you and do it'. So this fool's story was born.

I would like to thank all those who helped me along the way and who travelled with me around the world; it was a real pleasure. We rarely had arguments and that is perhaps down to my use of a saying which my good friend John Riordan always used in tight corners: 'be reasonable, see things my way'.

A huge thanks to Terry and Ann O'Sullivan and family for putting up with my visits to their house where Ann did a wonderful job of deciphering my scribble and typing every word of this book. To my publisher, Roz Crowley, at Onstream, my thanks for enjoyable days bringing this book to fruition.

To everyone who encouraged me to continue and to all those who are surprised that I could write so many words

(I was never known for my writing talent), here we are now!

I always feel that I was lucky to be born into a sporting family; I often wonder what other people do on Sundays. If by chance there is no match or sporting event to attend on a Sunday, I am completely lost. Thank God there are very few of those days.

My son Brendan and all my nephews and nieces are all so interested in sport that they have created their own list of achievements which add to my own pleasure: Brendan was a very good badminton player and represented Cork in both it and cross-country running; my nephews, Donal and Barry Murphy, have both won hurling All-Ireland medals with Cork, and always enjoyed the sideline support of their lovely sister Niamh; some of my brother Eamon's six children have represented Cork and Ireland in hurling and football; and my sister Kathleen's children have represented Kilkenny in hockey and camogie.

I count myself lucky that I can take to most sports. Early on when I was first posted as a garda in Ballyconnell and was basically stranded as I didn't have a car, I got into watching cricket on television. I found it hard to follow, except when one of the players hit a four or, better still, a six. I would like to have attended the 2007 Cricket World Cup in the West Indies as Ireland has qualified for the finals for the first time but, owing to the launch of this book, I had to miss it.

The BBC programme, *Pot Black,* got me interested in snooker, and horses and dog racing have always held a fascination for me. I have attended races in most of the tracks in Ireland from grand nationals in Fairyhouse to point-to-points locally. One of the best night's sports I ever enjoyed anywhere was the Irish Greyhound Derby in Shelbourne Park. I don't think I have experienced an atmosphere quite like it: the mass-anticipation is electric as the dogs are put in the traps ... the roar as the hare starts up, then the silence as the hare approaches the box ... the traps open and the place erupts for thirty seconds, the noise level is unbelievable.

I was in a pub in Watergrasshill lately when two fellows who I knew asked me to join them. We had a bit of banter as I told them that I would not associate myself with 'blow-ins'. One of these two men, John O'Connell, has lived in 'the Hill' for forty-five years, and the other, Dick Gardiner, is there thirty years. They asked me for my definition of a blow-in and I explained using the example of my sister, Kathleen, who has been living in Kilkenny for nearly forty years. She taught there, played camogie with Kilkenny, married a Kilkenny man, had six children, including Ciarán and Dáire, who both won All-Ireland medals with different Kilkenny teams, and is a member of Kilkenny County Council and is not considered a native. That, I said to my friends, is a good example of a blow-in. When asked where I am from, I always say that the only place in Ireland to be is from Watergrasshill. Here is the story of some of my exploits, starting on the Hill.

– I –

Childhood

My childhood was nothing special, not even to me. I was born the last of six children to Jim and Mary Ryan, in Watergrasshill (known as the Hill), Co. Cork. My father was one of thirteen Ryans from Smiths Road in Charleville. He worked for Sutton's Coals in Charleville, Mitchelstown, Cork and then Watergrasshill, where he met and fell in love with Mary O'Riordan, a native of Watergrasshill and the youngest of twelve children.

While courting and preparing to get married, the Ryans in Charleville objected to him marrying Mary, as they felt she was not good enough for him. Funnily enough, the O'Riordans didn't think Jim was good enough for her either, so Jim and Mary did what every young couple in love would do and, in spite of everyone, got married and spent over forty happy years together. They spent their honeymoon in Cork city, staying a night or two in the Ashley Hotel in Coburg Street, and then it was back to work and on to married life.

Their first born child was Eamon, followed by Mary, who died aged two, then Mick, followed by Kathleen and

My mother and father on their wedding day in 1945

Mary and – the best wine saved till last – I was born on 21 March 1954 in the Glenvera Nursing Home, Wellington Road, Cork, currently a refugee centre.

Our house in the village of Watergrasshill was home to my family and Aunt Hannah, my mother's sister, who moved in for a week shortly after my parents got married and stayed for sixty-five years, outliving both of them by fourteen years. We also had Bran, a blind dog, and a deaf cat called Billy who looked after one another.

Later my father bought Sutton's Depot in the Hill from where he sold animal feed, grass seed, coal, turf and manure. I used to deliver coal and turf around the village in my hand truck for him. Aunt Hannah would fill it into bags and we would be black from head to foot. Both those and the two-hundredweight bags of 10-10-20 fertiliser played havoc with my back. As the store was across the road from our house, Hannah was known to everyone who passed.

Hannah was a great one for the death notices and she took great pride in reading the deaths of people who were younger than her. She also kept an eye on any funeral of interest to the rest of the family. One such time was the funeral in Charleville of a Jimmy Ryan. In Charleville, there are Ryans all over the place and numerous Jimmy Ryans, some of whom were related to my father. At the time in Watergrasshill there were three Jim Ryans: my father, myself and Eamon and Pat's first born, which led to confusion. So Hannah announced the death of Jimmy Ryan, and the time and place of the ceremonies. She, my father and mother and their driver, son-in-law Tim Murphy, headed off for the funeral mass arriving in Charleville just in time. Hannah led the charge up the church and announced to one of the ushers that they were chief mourners and headed up to the top of the church. Halfway up the aisle they were met, you guessed it, by Jimmy Ryan, the man they thought they had come to bury. He said they were very good to have come down to the funeral as he thought my father would hardly know the deceased. Hannah never lived that one down. She outlived all of her family and remained in our house after the rest of us had all left home. She died in 1990 aged eighty-two.

There were only two young fellows of my age in the village at the time: me and Denis Murphy. We played, fought and made up with one another all the time. We had Goal to Goal matches in Coakley's Field, which was behind our house, and swam in the pond alongside dogs, cattle and sheep. The Hill is 1,000 feet above sea level and is prone to snow and frost so we also had great fun on the ice, with some even having bicycle races across it. We had the first flood-lit pitch in the country too, and the whole village would play a match under the three lights. Many's the great game was played up and down the main street, which was also the main Cork to Dublin road.

My first day in school will stay in my memory forever. My sister, Kathleen, and cousin, Mick Riordan, were detailed to take me to school. All went well and I was happy to go the 100 yards down the street until, that is, I came to the gates of the school. Like a stubborn cow, I baulked, and all they could do was bring me back home to my mother, who appeared to be very sympathetic to my cause and told the others to go back to school themselves. She sat at the bottom of the stairs with me on her lap, then turned me over and walloped my backside. After that I never had a problem going to school again. This was the same staircase where from the top I often 'said mass' while my two sisters were the altar girls. We made the vestments out of newspaper.

In school I had a number of different teachers – Mrs O'Connell, a lovely, gentle woman, and Mrs Buckley, who slapped us with the ruler. It was she who caught me kissing Breda Kiely in the class one day. It took me a long time before I tried it again after the punishment I got for that kiss. The head teacher was Master McCarthy, or Dan Mac as he was known. He was a gentleman who was uneasy talking about the Civil War as, like most of his generation, he had lived through that era and had to pick a side. That was a strange thing about school in those days: we were taught about every invasion and everything that happened from 0 to 1916, but very little about what happened in this country after that.

Then I had a certain Mr Ryan – my brother, Eamon – who taught me for a while. It was quite awkward as we slept in the same room and sometimes in the same bed but at school he was my teacher. But generally, school in the Hill was good. Each day at playtime there would be a big match between Cork and Kerry and it may seem strange, but somehow Cork always managed to win these matches.

There was a farmyard near our house in the Hill and I spent a lot of time there. It has been said to me that one day my mother was looking for me and I was found up in the farm asleep on top of one of the sows. When not up in the farm I would be next door, with a lady called Liz Connell, who had a small one-up-one-down house where we all used to gather and learned how to 'smoke' paper;

this was where you rolled up newspaper tight so it looked like a cigarette, then you lit it and blew it out again, but kept a spark on the end which created the smoke. I spent a lot of time at another neighbour's house as well, with Batt and Mrs Hayes and her sister Miss Manning. They were very generous and would give me a few pennies for doing odd jobs for them. They also had a lovely garden in which they took great pride.

Our parish priest at that time was Fr Lambe who, when he was a very young priest, had a run-in with his bishop in Tipperary and was sent to Cape Clear as punishment. He remained there for forty years until he came to the Hill. I was an altar boy at a time when all masses were said in Latin. Fr Lambe was a radical in his time. When the Dublin traffic drove through the village at speed, he proposed that the people build a wall across the top of the village to stop them speeding. He was serious about it, even though at times cars found it hard to climb up to the village with the snow and ice on the road. In fact at times, when the lorries would eventually climb up the hill to the village, their engines would be so overheated they would have to stop outside our house. We could feel the whole house shaking.

At one stage the council put down this new anti-ice tar at the Fermoy side of the village and when the first freeze came, no cars were able to get out of the village because it was too slippy. The tar was a disaster and it all had to be taken up again.

Fr Lambe was in the Hill for a good number of years

and, when he got older and his memory started to go, he used to say mass in the oratory in his house. I was his regular altar boy and would go up to his house for 9 a.m. mass. He would start the mass, get as far as the epistle, then go back and start again, then maybe get to the gospel and go back to the start again. After a bit of help from me and his housekeeper we would eventually get to the end of mass but it was often half eleven by the time I got back to school. Fr Lambe was a great man and the elderly people in the parish still speak fondly of him.

My father was a handy sportsman. He played a lot of handball, got to a Tipperary county final, but had to give a walkover as my sister Kathleen decided she was going to arrive into the world that day. He never forgave her. It is also said that he won a North Cork minor medal with Charleville when he was in his mid-twenties, which he never denied nor confirmed.

When he arrived in the Hill he got involved in the local club as a selector so it was inevitable that his offspring would get involved. Wasn't he proud when his son Mick, my brother, who was a classy hurler, made the Cork minor team in 1961 and played in front of the biggest crowd to ever witness a Munster final in Limerick. They were beaten but he later made the Cork intermediate team. It was thought that, but for the rule that clerical students could not play sport for teams outside the college after summer holidays, he would have been good enough for the Cork senior team.

The highlight of the Ryans' sporting times was when my brother Eamon made the Cork senior football team in the 1960s and played in the All-Ireland final in 1967 which Cork lost to Meath. A few weeks after that, my sister Kathleen played for Cork in the All-Ireland junior camogie final. Unfortunately they didn't win either.

As all the family was involved, my interest in sport developed at a very young age. In those days there was very little television or any of today's other distractions. The hurling pitch was across the road and the dressing rooms were in our coal store; of course there were no showers in those days. The home team changed in the clean store, while the opposition changed in the coal store which also held animal rations and fertilisers. We kept the most comfortable store for ourselves. On one Sunday, for some misdemeanour, perhaps it was back-answering my mother, I was put up to my room for the evening. There was a match on in the pitch and from my room all I could see was the back of the top goalposts. It was a long evening and I made sure I didn't offend again. At the time the pitch, now Priory Court, was owned by the O'Mahony family who kept their cattle in the field. We had great craic throwing the cow dung at each other. Often we would get home and have to stand under the cold tap outside the back door before being allowed inside.

Leaving Watergrasshill National School having, to everyone's surprise, passed the Primary Cert., I headed to Fermoy CBS. As there was very little hurling or football I only lasted two years at this school and went to Coláiste Chríost

Rí in Cork. It was suggested that I should go to Farranferris College but even at that stage I was wise enough to know that entry as a day boy could very easily lead to being a boarder. I liked my freedom so somehow I convinced my parents that Chríost Rí was a better choice and dodged that bullet. I settled there very quickly as I got on the Harty Cup panel and stayed on that team for four years, winning no medals or titles. I was also on the senior football team but, after a dispute with the trainer over leaving training early to get a necessary bus home, I was dropped off the team and panel. It got so bad between us that I was only a sub on the junior team. In the Munster semi-final in Lismore, we were down two points with two minutes to go, so he put me on and I scored two points to level the game and the match went to extra time. Before that extra time started I was brought off the pitch again and did not get back on the team. The senior team went on to meet and beat St Malachy's from Derry, whose team included Martin O'Neill. Instead, I got drunk that day.

I started drinking very early in life, perhaps as early as the age of five, and any time my uncles came to visit us they would take me to O'Mahony's, the local pub. They would give me porter in small glasses and try to get me drunk. When farmers came to pay, my father would get the end of their bottles of porter for me. At confirmation I took the pledge, a promise to keep away from alcohol until the age of twenty-one, which seems to be less fashionable these days. That only lasted about two years. I was the only country boy on the football team and had access to money as my mother had a money box over the fireplace which I was able to get at. I was very popular with the lads as I would 'lend' them a few bob for the drink.

The hurling team was a different matter. No matter what I did, I couldn't get off the team. Even when I got expelled, which happened a few times, I was always allowed back in the evening for training.

As I got older, I had the use of my father's car. A few of us would sneak out a window at school and head to Kinsale or Crosshaven for an hour or two and get back in time for training. Once you were there for the role-call you could get away with being missing later. After four years on the senior team all I had to show were two O'Callaghan Cup medals (Cork Colleges), though that team was one of the best of the colleges around at the time and the rest of the team members went on to play for Cork at some level or other.

I also took an interest in other sports like soccer and rugby. I often mitched school to go to see Cork Hibernians or Celtic when they would be playing in Turners Cross or Flower Lodge, now Pairc Uí Rinn. Both teams were going well at the time. Hibs had great players: Dave Bacuzzi, Noel O'Mahony, Fada Sheehan, John Herrick and the great Miah Dennehy, Dave Wiggington and Tony Marsden, to name just a few. Celtic had the likes of John Carroll, Noel Miller, Dinny Allen and, of course, the great Carl Davenport. They were fantastic times in Cork soccer and it was great to be part of the enthusiastic crowds going to the matches, despite the ban which prevented GAA spectators going to watch soccer, rugby, hockey and cricket.

The first big game I saw was on Tuesday, 3 July 1973. I got a loan of my father's car, a Morris Minor, and met my sister Kathleen in Durrow. She had moved to Kilkenny and helped to form St Patrick's Majorettes, which were the first majorettes in the country. We headed off to Dublin where they were playing before, and during the interval in, a charity match for UNICEF and the Irish Cancer Society between Shamrock Rovers Ireland and Brazil, the world champions. The Ireland XI consisted of players from both sides of the border including Pat Jennings, Martin O'Neill, Derek Dougan, John Giles, Paddy Mulligan and Don Givens. It was a great match, which Brazil won 4-3. Pat Jennings was an inspired player that day – what a game for your first international! By now I really had the bug of international football but little did I realise that I would follow this game to the four corners of the world and back.

Having the car going to school was handy but it often got me into trouble. We had maths first thing on a Monday morning with Mr Daly. One particular Monday I was suffering from a hangover so decided I would not be able to cope with him. I arrived in time and made my way into the toilets where I met up with others in the same boat. Coming up to the end of class time I made my way to the cloakroom area near the classroom, waited for the noise of the door to open and give Mr Daly a chance to leave and disappear. When I thought it was safe I entered the classroom and who was the first to meet me only Mr Daly.

He asked me where I had been.

'The bus broke down,' I said.

'Oh,' he said, 'was your car stolen last night?'

'I don't think so, why?' I replied.

'Well,' he said, 'your name has been called over the tannoy since nine o'clock this morning.'

In my hurry to get into school unnoticed, I had parked my car in front of the gateway and blocked the entrance so people couldn't come in or out of the school. In future I made sure I was more careful where I left the car. Somehow or other, I didn't get punished. Mr Daly seemed to see the funny side.

When I arrived in Chríost Rí, I did Latin and commerce, as well as other subjects, but if you wanted to continue with commerce, you had to do Spanish as well. We had a lady teacher for Spanish and from the first day we had a personality clash. We did not see eye to eye so I hated Spanish and could not come to terms with it at all. I did badly in it in the Intermediate Certificate, and in the Leaving Certificate had one look at the paper and walked out of the exam after fifteen minutes.

I left Coláiste Chríost Rí with no Harty medal, no Corn Uí Mhuire, no Inter. Cert. and no Leaving Cert. When the results of the Leaving Cert. arrived, I was on crutches with a broken foot, sustained in an under-21 hurling match. I went into a hole in the field awkwardly and heard the crack. I went down and our First Aid people – the fellows with the bottle of water – came in to see what was wrong. I told them I thought my foot was broken. I still remember what one of them said to me: 'Ryan, there is f... all wrong with you; you are only looking for attention. Play On!' Fool that I was, I did, and later that night ended up in hospital. I was in plaster for five weeks and, with a poor final score, I didn't get a whole lot of TLC.

Of course, if I had studied, I probably would have done well academically, but I used to take our dog down to the pond and teach him how to swim and catch eels instead. To make up for lost time at school I would buy the synopsis version of books and read them – a good idea on principle, but one which just didn't work. Perhaps if I had read them, I would have had some chance.

While still at school I worked in the store at home, as well as working as a barman in O'Mahony's. I also worked as a relief postman in the Hill area which was divided up into two sections for the two postmen. The funny thing was that the postmen took holidays but spent their time watching that I or the other relief postmen did not go back to the post office too early. When they were working, they would usually pop in home on their way back to the post office so it wouldn't look good if we got back sooner than them. Everyday they would be in the village waiting for me to return, which sometimes was a long wait as I had a number of my own safe houses that I would go to and have the breakfast. This suited me perfectly, as often, after being out all night, I would sit in a soft chair and fall asleep for a few hours. I always delivered the letters though, maybe not at the time they were expected but they always got there. The routes were about twenty odd

Left to right: my siblings Eamon, Mary, Mick and Kathleen

miles on a big heavy bike so no-one could blame me for taking a rest along the way.

Holidays were enjoyed in my cousins', the Riordans' house in Skahana, a mile down the road, which we all loved. We would cut the silage, then pound it by riding the horse up and down over it. We also drew in the hay with a horse and cart. It was here that I learned how to smoke at the early age of ten; No. 6 was the brand.

– 2 –

Templemore

In April 1964, when I was ten years old, one of the most brutal and famous murders in this country took place in Watergrasshill. Mr and Mrs George Applebe were asleep in their bed at home, about a mile from the village, when they were butchered by a former workman. Mr Applebe died but his wife survived her awful ordeal. It was a Friday night/Saturday morning when the news broke and the whole area was terrified as it was one of the few murders in the country that year. For us Catholics in those days it was a mortal sin to go into a Protestant church and I can still picture myself on the day of the funeral standing across the road from the church, afraid to venture over.

It was the first time I had taken any notice of the gardaí. The murder was solved and the culprit, Jimmy Ellis, who used to work with Mr Applebe, was sentenced to life in prison. At that time we had three gardaí in the village – Paddy Brown and Dick Meehan, who lived near me in the village, and Sergeant Michael O'Connor, who lived in the station. Other gardaí would come to the village from time to time, including Liam Harkin, with whom I later served.

These gentlemen left a big impression on me and I said to myself that when I grew up I would become a guard.

True to my word, in 1972 I sat the entrance exam, met with the local sergeant, Dan Kennedy, and did the interview with the superintendent, Mattie Ryan, in his car on the way to Garda Paddy Brown's funeral.

I must have done all right as I was accepted into the Garda Síochána and on Wednesday, 6 March 1974, my sister Mary drove me to Templemore and in through those big gates. We assembled in the hall, all ninety of us, with our relations. We were sworn in and Garda James Mariano Ryan was given the Reg. No. 19496D. I had got the middle name Mariano because when I was born, the parish priest at the time took a shine to me and wanted me to be called after a great rugby player called Marty Cunningham. My father would not allow it to be my first name because he wanted me to be called after him and didn't want me to be called after a rugby player. He compromised and gave it to me as my second name, but in Italian.

I was now the first generation garda in both the Ryan and Riordan clan and only the third at that stage from the Hill; John B. O'Sullivan and John O'Regan were before me and, surprisingly, after me there wasn't another for nearly twenty-five years, when Michelle O'Leary joined. It was surprising that so few applied because of the very first garda recruits in 1922, two of them, Richard Meehan and John Roche, lived long and healthily into their late nineties in the Hill.

Back in the great hall at Templemore we signed our

lives away; I signed any paper that was put in front of me – pension, tax and numerous subscriptions. In Roches Stores I had been earning £12 per week, and that included working till 9 p.m. on Friday nights. My first pay package in Templemore was £32 a week, so I nearly trebled my money. When the formalities were finished we were shown to our dormitories, our home for the next eighteen weeks, or so we thought.

My two roommates were Tom Stroker from Roscommon and Frank McCooey from Monaghan. We got on well and all got into the swing of things. However, like any new recruit we stood out, marching awkwardly which felt even worse as we hadn't yet got our uniforms.

The first evening we were all sent down to the guard room at the front gate, where a barber waited to attack each of us in turn with his razor. My head of curly hair vanished and even in the mild March weather I felt the cold. This was when everyone had long hair so it was a huge change for all of us

The following day we were introduced to police studies, Irish and a whole lot of different subjects dealing with garda work. As we discovered later, a lot of what we learned was of little use afterwards; common sense would play a greater part in our lives as gardaí. We learned definitions of dangerous driving, public places, powers of arrest and custody, which at the time were boring but were to come in handy later.

We were then issued with our uniform: very woolly pants which were very warm in the winter, but cruelly hot in the summer; and shirts with detachable collars held in place by studs. You always knew a garda, not by the haircut, but by the stud mark on his throat. These shirts were very popular with women, as when we were finished with them, they used them as nighties. We also had the tunic: an outer coat worn over the shirt as a jacket.

The uniform changed over the years to become more practical: we were given lighter shirts; allowed to let the tunics off during the summertime and wear sleeveless jumpers instead. We also had what was called a Grey Coat (I don't know why as it was blue), which was knee length. I later turned one of them into a stylish Crombie coat by taking off the buttons and getting a dressmaker to take off the epaulettes and narrow the lapels. We also had massive waterproof coats which, once they got wet, weighed a ton. The water would run down onto your pants if you didn't have the waterproof pull-ups. They took an age to put on and when you had all that gear on you sweated like a pig. We eventually got the now official jumper, patrol jacket, short-sleeved shirts, summer pants and tunic.

Unlike nowadays we had to stay in the depot most weekends during training and only got home for about three weekends. As few of us had cars we might as well have been in prison as it was so difficult to get out of Templemore. One Sunday, after our march to and from mass, it took me one and a half hours to get a lift out of there and another hour out of Thurles. I gave up and ended up getting the train.

As I had a few near misses from drowning – most

notably in Dunquinn, Co. Kerry – I had a fear of water for many years, so when the pool became part of the course, I froze and could not master it. It didn't help when one of the instructors made me go up on the high board and walk out to the end. I refused to jump. Another time he made me jump off the side of the pool, which I did, but banged my head off the side wall. While I didn't go unconscious, I felt groggy and sick and it was as good an excuse as any not to get back into the pool. I still cannot swim.

I was lucky I was not drinking at this stage. At the age of eighteen I realised I had already started to depend on drink. Most days at lunchtime in school I would go to the pub down the road and have a few pints, so I often came back to school with a strong smell of drink from me, and had to keep well away from teachers. Likewise at home I had to be careful. Perhaps they knew, but it was never mentioned.

I could see I had a problem and decided that the only way was to give it up completely. It was a huge decision for an eighteen-year-old. All my friends were drinking but they never put pressure on me to continue.

Smoking was another of my bad habits. I had my first cigarette when I was about six or seven with Mick Sullivan. His mother had a shop in the village and he would invite us all to the Meadow Field to sample some smokes that he had 'acquired' at home. As usual, my sister Kathleen spotted the smoke and told my mother (sisterly love how are you), and I got myself another red bottom. I didn't smoke again until one day my cousin Mick Riordan gave me a cigarette. From then on I was hooked and at one stage was up to eighty a day. Eventually, about fifteen years ago, when a lot of people were going off them, I managed to give them up ... and added four stone to my weight.

Not drinking was especially important to me later on. Templemore was a very boring place and there wasn't a lot to do in the evenings so I could have got into real trouble. Instead I used to work in the college shop in the evenings, and was involved in the college hurling, football and soccer teams, which was a great experience as we had to play the other divisions in Munster. We were fairly fit and most of the divisional teams were made up of fellows a lot older and heavier than us. But they made up for this lack of fitness with cuteness and cunning. I was on the ground more often than not as the ball approached. They knew how to slow us young fellows down to their pace.

About six weeks into our training, we were told that all weekend passes were withdrawn and that we would be going on duty to Castlebar, Mayo, for the funeral of a hunger striker, Michael Gaughan. There was real excitement within the recruits because this was going to be real garda work. We got up at four on the Sunday morning, had breakfast, and were all bussed to Castlebar, where we were briefed. The recruits were to be near the grave and we were told that, if he appeared, we were to arrest Daithí O'Connell, who was wanted and was on the run. The irony of it was that most of us had not even heard of Daithí O'Connell, let alone knew what he looked like. I remember seeing this man get up and make a great speech and learned later that in fact it was Mr O'Connell, who then disappeared into the crowd. I often wondered after that whether or not they really wanted to arrest him. Why did they put 100 gardaí near him who would not know him, while the seasoned gardaí were outside the graveyard?

We arrived back at the depot in the early hours of Monday morning and were told we could have Monday off. On the Tuesday, our instructor, Reg Barrett, brought us into the gym, lined us all up and proceeded to show us how to use the baton. He told us what we could have done if anything had gone wrong on Sunday – a bit late. Lucky for us nothing much had happened, except for being subjected to all sorts of abuse and insults. However, we were naive enough to think that they were not meant for us, but for the older gardaí.

While in the depot we put on a concert. Before I joined I used to do a mime act of Elvis and some other rock stars, so I did this on the night. Before I knew where I was, I was doing my party piece, along with other recruits, at parish concerts in different halls in mid-Tipperary. I had a sky blue Elvis style suit – big lapels, bell-bottom trousers, white shirt and big tie. While it looked quite formal, once the music started, I would loosen the tie, open the coat, take off the coat and then the tie which I threw to the side of the stage. Finally I would open the shirt all the way down to my waist. I had a show-off body at that stage and had a lot of fun moving my hips like the King. It went down very well. Everyone went a bit wild, cheering every move and of course I loved the attention.

Passing out, 1974

I was never a great one for study but passed my first two exams without difficulty. As we approached the final exam we were told that a new man would set the final exam paper. We knew this meant a stiff exam but little did we realise that we were to be the guinea pigs for generations to come. Many were to fail in the future owing to this inspector's ego trip.

We sat the exams and waited for the results; usually, the results would be known on the Monday before the Thursday of the 'passing out'. Monday came and went, then Tuesday, and we eventually got the results on Wednesday evening at 4.50 p.m. As predicted, ten, including me, had failed. It was too late to stop all our relations from turning up for the ceremony. I was nominated to meet the chief superintendent to discuss the situation of the 'Templemore Ten'. We worked out a deal where we would sit the exam again in a fortnight and he more or less guaranteed we would all pass. Then I had the problem of telling my proud parents.

I couldn't tell them the truth so I told them that as I was going to the border, I had been picked to do a bomb disposal course *and wouldn't get my certificate until after that*. There were no parents more proud of their son than mine. We had a great day and night in Templemore and I don't think I told them the truth for a long time. The ten of us hung around the depot for the fortnight, sat the exam and all passed and headed off to our new work as servants of the state.

– 3 –
Ballyconnell

Generally speaking, about ten days to two weeks before you pass out of the depot you are given your station. The normal thing was the passing out was on a Thursday and you headed off to your new station on the Friday morning. It was a very sad Friday morning for the Templemore Ten as we watched the rest of our class head off to their respective stations, full of the joys of life, while we had at least another fortnight to wait.

My station was to be Ballyconnell, Co. Cavan, in what was known as the war zone. I checked atlases and maps but found no trace of Ballyconnell. I eventually found it tucked up to the border to Fermanagh on the road from Cavan to Enniskillen.

We finished the 'bomb disposal' course, passed the repeat exam, and the ten of us headed off to our different stations. First we got a train to Dublin, then a few of us took the bus to Cavan, where we were met by a mule (garda slang for a garda) in a patrol car who was to deliver us to our stations. I was enjoying the spin out of Cavan and onto Belturbet – our first time in the area – when a call came out over the radio system that there was a bomb on the bridge in Belturbet. I asked the driver where that was and he replied, 'We are on it that bridge right now!' I certainly wished I'd done a bomb disposal course then. Our driver got out of the car, walked over to a suitcase that was sitting on the bridge, caught it and flung it over the bridge. He then came back to the car and to me who was shitting bricks at my first introduction to 'The War'. 'Them effing hoaxes,' he said. I agreed with his sentiments.

On arrival in Ballyconnell, I could see straight away how it had won the Tidy Towns competition a few years previously; it had a most scenic entrance and main street. I arrived at the station, which had a permanent checkpoint outside where I was to spend many, many hours on duty. We met the sergeant, Jack Fadden, who lived in one of the two agency houses attached to the station.

Ballyconnell was a district HQ which meant it had a superintendent and inspector attached to it. The super was Jim Brogan, a Dubliner and father of Dublin footballers Bernard and Jim; this was handy because when the pressure was on you could always sidetrack him by talking about football.

Next on the agenda was to settle in with Bridie and Enda O'Brien, who owned a chipper and housed numerous mules. I was made very welcome straight away and am still in contact with them. It was a lovely big double house, and we all had our own rooms. This was to be my home for the next three years

On my first night, to break me in, one of the lads took

me to a dance in Ballinamore. On the way home from the dance, he gave a lift to a friend of his who lived in the next village down the road, Derrylin, Co. Fermanagh. On the way down the four-mile stretch, they told me about all the people who had been murdered on that stretch of road. While having tea at 4 a.m. in this house in Northern Ireland, I learned that in the house next door, which was also a butcher's shop, the two brothers who owned it had been killed and their bodies hung up in the big walk-in fridge and left there over the weekend. I remembered reading about these murders. It was time to get out of there and face the journey back to my lodgings – a trip I made many times after. This first night really tested my vocation.

For the next few days, I was taken around in the squad car and shown the area. The road past the station was a concession road (a road without a customs post), and it led to Derrylin and on to Enniskillen. I soon got to know the area fairly well. A number of towns – Belturbet, Swanlinbar, Ballinamore, Carrigallen – were stations in Ballyconnell district. There was also a sub-station in Bawnboy, which was manned by Joe Walsh. The Ballyconnell district car was always busy as we had the army with us doing checkpoints. The army had a barracks in Ballyconnell where they would transfer for two months at a time from Athlone, but it was never they who went on patrol with us. Instead, a different unit would arrive every night from Longford, while the Ballyconnell unit patrolled elsewhere.

The first three officers I came across had all been in

school with me in Cork, so it was easy to settle in. Some heard that I could play football so I was signed up to play with the local team, Kildallen. I must have played well enough as I was promoted to the senior team, Woodford Gaels. We also had a station team, which we fielded in a tournament between all the stations in the district. Being all border stations there were high numbers of young fit members in each station. I was also playing at home in Cork which meant I was actually illegal in GAA terms. In effect, I was playing on four teams, all GAA, but for two in Cork and two in Cavan at the same time.

When Terry O'Sullivan, a garda from Midleton, arrived in Ballyconnell we introduced the sport of road bowling, which involved throwing a 28 ounce ball of iron down the road. Imagine the looks we got as we headed towards the border throwing this iron ball! The locals did not take to it at all, preferring the game of skittles which I had not seen played before but which is popular in a number of areas in the country. Skittles is played by throwing short lengths of timber at a circle a few yards away and trying to knock down the timbers in that circle which each have a different value; a bit like ten-pin bowling outdoors. Our bowling didn't take on but Terry and I had a good few enjoyable Sundays playing.

My interest in soccer continued and I often went to Dublin, Sligo or Ballybofey to watch Cork teams playing in the league. I also started following the horses and greyhounds and in our time off Terry and I could be found in most racetracks within a two-hour drive of Ballyconnell.

We made and lost a lot of money in this time, but survived.

Money management has never been my strong point. When I first arrived in Ballyconnell I was hardly out of the car when this fellow got me to take out a life policy which he said would be worth a fortune in thirty years time. Sucker that I was, I signed. I also took out another policy with a man who used to call to my parents. Later I decided they were a waste of time so I went to cash them in. The one I took out in Ballyconnell barely gave me back what I had paid in, while the other one told me I hadn't paid in two years. The payments had been stopped by someone, not by me or the bank, so I got nothing worthwhile back.

That was it with insurance policies until I was on a checkpoint one night with a very wise garda who told me I should take out a policy that would mature just after I retired. I enquired and took out a policy that was going to give me all this money when it matured. When I retired I got my own money back plus a tiny bonus – I suppose it was better than the returns I got from my dabbling in shares. In 1987, I had bought shares in a company which were supposed to make me a fortune. They might have, but for Black Friday when the share market collapsed. In 1989, I bought others, which were again going to make me millions. In 1991 and 1993 I bought more and still have them, neat and tidy in a folder. Worthless. I'm a gambler and a sucker for a fast buck. I should have learned over the years that there's no such thing but I enjoy the buzz of being a shareholder, even in worthless companies.

I was also in a syndicate for a horse but it broke a leg and had to be put down. Another horse was bought but he too had to be assassinated. I was part-owner of a dog which was eventually sold for less than we bought it, and only started winning races while in the hands of new owners. Then at work a lot of us got together and bought a good dog. He won a few races and we were offered a lot of money for him. We resisted. Guess what? He started to lose races and we eventually sold him also for less then we paid for him. I mention all this as a warning to those who might be tempted to ask my advice on shares, life policies, dogs or horses.

While in Ballyconnell I went to my first international abroad: London, 1976, against the old enemy. I went over for a week as the fare was cheaper than going for a few days. Of course I didn't take into account the boredom factor or indeed the B&B price, so I walked around London for a week thinking I had saved money. The match itself was memorable for a great tackle on Kevin Keegan by a seventeen-year-old David O'Leary, getting his first cap.

In later years I was to travel over to London for many Irish matches. One in particular was in the 1980s, at the time when Barry McGuigan was in full flight in his boxing career. I went to Wembley Stadium to see a game and left with about ten minutes to go as McGuigan was boxing in the Wembley Arena. I went down towards the arena and could hear the cheering inside. The touts had the only remaining tickets and they wanted £100 sterling each. I was just about to hand over the money when a man came running out and announced that McGuigan had won by a knockout in the first round. A lucky save.

My next trip was to Bulgaria for the European Games in Sofia. I discovered that it was £188 to get there for four days and only £187 for a fortnight, so to save £1 I went for the fortnight. It was my first of many visits to Bulgaria as Ireland went through a stage where we seemed to play there all the time. This particular game was the one in which four players were sent off, two from each side – Noel Campbell and Mick Martin from Ireland – and we lost the game. There were 80,000 at the match, including 500 Irish, and the police kept the 79,500 Bulgarians in the stadium after the match so we could get away safely. Amazing!

While I was there, walking along the beach one day, I came across a building site with shuttering around it. I was curious so I walked up to see through a small gap in the laths. I saw something that I thought was only possible in films, which was a lot of women prisoners in balls and chains. I never discovered why they were there but Bulgaria was still a communist country and it wasn't easy to get an explanation.

Another time going to Sofia, we flew with Balkan Airlines and a great sing-song started up. I was heading up to the front of the plane when I looked and saw that the plane was flying away on autopilot. Shortly after, the plane hit an air pocket and dropped a huge distance. The pilot quickly regained his concentration and took hold of the controls. The sing-song stopped too; we all got a fright but no harm was done.

That was the time when the Irish supporters were marshalled in the pouring rain into and around the stadium with a row of police at either side of us. I was standing with my Irish scarf in one hand when I saw a young fellow coming towards me, past the police cordon. He put something into my hand and took my scarf. It was a huge Bulgarian flag, which I still have. We got drowned wet that night and lost the game as well, which was for the Euro '88 qualifiers. Scotland later did us a favour and beat Bulgaria to let us into Euro '88.

The next big fight I attended was the 1995 World Championship at Millstreet between Steve Collins and Chris Eubank. What a night it was, what atmosphere! I was lucky enough to secure tickets in the middle of the arena, just below the television cameras. The craic and good humour around Millstreet and on the way up to Green Glens was great but nothing compared to the electric atmosphere in the arena in the lead up to the fight. Eubank made his usual entrance, arriving from the roof on a huge motorbike. Collins made his entrance accompanied by Tony Quinn, his guru. The fight was a hard slog but Collins won to make it a night I will remember forever.

My time in Ballyconnell was great craic, both in the station and in the house. Our landlady, Bridie, was an awful 'caffler' and was always playing tricks on us, as we did on her. You might just be sitting down to your tea and for some reason or other be called away, and when you would come back and be gasping for a mouthful of tea Bridie would have emptied the salt cellar into the cup. A mouthful was pretty disgusting. The house was full of cockroaches and when we'd come over for our break, if we didn't turn on the light we would crush them on the floor of the kitchen with our feet. Turning on the light and seeing them all scatter was just as bad.

There were twelve gardaí and one bank official staying in the house and we all got on well. We travelled a lot together, except when coming home on a Thursday at 2 p.m. when there would be a mass exodus from Ballyconnell. My first brand new car was a bright yellow Ford Escort, WID 307. As it was difficult enough to get out of Ballyconnell, the car gave me great freedom.

There was a lot of activity in the Ballyconnell area, with shootings on the border, bombs and bomb hoaxes. One evening the British were doing a checkpoint near the border when the Provos started shooting down on them. The Irish army went above the Provos and we went between them all. The Provos pulled out, so we had a situation where the Irish army was firing down on the British and we were in between. The Provos would always come at 9.45 p.m. – a most inconvenient time as we finished our shift at 10 p.m.

One night I was driving the squad car with Dominic Flynn, a new recruit, and we got a call that there was a checkpoint at the border on our side. We were dispatched down to see who was patrolling it. I drove down to the checkpoint and past the uniformed men, turned the car around and drove back past them again. I told Dominic I was getting out to see who these uniformed men were and warned him to keep the radio in his hand; if he heard anything suspicious he was to call for help. I got out and walked back the road and my relief was instant when I heard the British accent. These men had arrived in Northern Ireland that morning, were given a map and told to go out and set up a checkpoint. They had strayed about 300 yards into the South, so I herded them back across the border and that was that. No international incident. It used to make me smile when you would hear about British incursions into the South and questions being asked in the Dáil. It seemed acceptable for the same British to fly into Cork to help a boat or some other vessel in trouble. I found it very opportunist and hypocritical.

Every Thursday there was a market in Enniskillen and great bargains were to be had. Despite the fact that the gardaí were not supposed to go into the North for security reasons, mules, custom officers and army shopped there for butter, car radios, petrol and tyres which were all much cheaper in the North. With all the Cork and Kerry accents around, it was like being in Patrick Street in Cork. We were all well received in Enniskillen and no-one took much notice; after all we were adding greatly to the town's economy. I was in a pub one night in the town when drinks were sent down to me, first by a Protestant, then by a Catholic. It was satisfying to be accepted by both sides and I was comfortable there.

We had many close calls on the border, particularly on the most dangerous concession roads in the North, which neither the British, the RUC nor ourselves could go on as they zig-zagged in and out of the North/South and so were a haven for Provo activists.

In 1973 the Provos went on a campaign of blowing up border crossings to disrupt the locals. One of these was the main Cavan/Enniskillen road at Labbacally Bridge, and it made the road impassable. This resulted in local farmers having to drive up to twenty miles to get to the other half of their farms.

One such person who had a business in the North was Sean Quinn, a regular poker player in the station. He had a quarry in Teemore but would draw his gravel up through our checkpoint and on through a concession road. This was not acceptable to Customs who expected him to travel about twenty miles to reach his destination of three miles. He would flout the law and every so often Customs would seize his lorry and he would have to buy it back from them – a real cat and mouse game. It did not stop his business growing though and now he has a huge empire.

I had a lucky escape on that road one night on my way back from Enniskillen at about 4 a.m. I came across two milk churns in the middle of the road and, while I thought about moving them, I was too tired to stop so kept on going and went to bed. I awoke a few hours later to be told that two British army soldiers had been blown up moving the churns on the road.

One night we arrested a local, let's call him Paddy. This

fellow fancied himself as a tough Provo. This time he was in for nothing related to the 'Cause', probably something to do with drink. He was quiet in his cell for a while but then started roaring and shouting. The cells in Ballyconnell were down a corridor at the end of the building, near the back door and the super's office. On the door was a small latch for checking the prisoners. I was in the day room with others when I smelled smoke coming down the corridor. Paddy's cell was on fire. We put out the fire and, though we had already done so, searched Paddy for matches. We took off his wellingtons, placed them outside the cell, and returned to the day room. Soon Paddy started roaring again. The cell was on fire again, this time not from Paddy setting fire to papers, but to his mattress. We put out the fire, this time with so much water that even Paddy got wet. He continued to roar and then went quiet.

When you have a prisoner, you have to check them every half hour so we were glad he was staying quiet for a few minutes and that there was no more smoke. Ten minutes after our last check, we heard a roaring on the roadway outside the station. It was Paddy: 'I'll see ye all in the morning boys,' he shouted and took off across the fields in the dark of the night. We didn't manage to catch him that night but re-arrested him the following morning. He got a great kick out of it and indeed we did too. I still don't know how he managed to get out through the cell door. I do know that he had the matches in the fold of his trouser leg. It was an entertaining night in Ballyconnell.

The Cavan area was a great dancing county, with dances

most nights of the week; Rockcarry, Bawnboy, Longford Arms, Belturbet and Ballinamore were all favourite spots. Droves of people would come through the checkpoint going to these dances and it passed the night away fairly well for us. They were all used to the drill at the checkpoint: as long as you stopped you were waved on. Our shift would be for eight hours on these checkpoints but you could be asked to work overtime; sixteen hours was fairly exhausting but the extra money compensated us. It could be pretty tedious.

One night I was station orderly (SO) and one of the lads was on the checkpoint. He spent most of the night with me, waving through the Venetian blinds in the station for cars to move on. All the cars obeyed his commands except one car that would not move. He went to the door and shouted at the car to drive on. Still no budge. It was about 2 a.m. and he eventually went out to the car. It was the super and inspector in a car we hadn't recognised. Words were spoken and after that we all made sure we stayed very near the checkpoint.

At one stage the divisional team was playing in the All-Ireland Garda Championship. Our chief super was Brendan Lynch, who had played for Roscommon, and he appointed Mick Higgins, the great Cavan footballer, in charge of our team. Cavan/Monaghan had never won the All-Ireland, and an all-out effort was being made to win it so there were no excuses for missing training. One day I was on overtime on the checkpoint. Training was at 5 p.m. in Clones followed by a match against Monaghan senior team. We had no inter-county players but we had a very even team. I was relieved of my checkpoint duty by another guard, also on overtime, went to training in Clones, arrived back to work at 9.30 p.m. and continued my checkpoint duty till 10 p.m. I suppose I was one of the first professional GAA players as I got my eight hours overtime as well! Our training paid off as we went on to win the All-Ireland in Croke Park against a star-studded Cork team.

In Ballyconnell we used to get a lot of temporary sergeants who were newly promoted and were sent to the border for six or twelve months to learn the ropes and to make them sorry for ever going for promotion. Most of them came up from Cork or Kerry, some from Dublin, including a lovely man named Ben McKenna who was also a great cyclist. Ben had won the Rás Tailtain some years previous and it was not unusual for him to cycle to Dublin or Belfast from Ballyconnell after work. Another man to come up from Limerick was Martin Brown, who got promoted in his thirtieth year in the gardaí, which was unusual. Martin was big into the greyhounds and as a number of the men were also into them, he felt very much at home.

I was never a great one for raiding pubs. I would go into them and get the people to leave if I thought they or the publican were abusing the situation. I always thought that it was a worse punishment to make someone leave a drink or two or three behind them than to ask them for their names and addresses. Nine out of ten would give me a wrong name anyway. But one night the sergeant got it into his head that he wanted to raid a particular pub which the sergeant-in-charge (IC) used to drink in as well as a whole lot of Northerners. I wasn't too happy to be going with him as I would have known most of the people but I had no other choice. I took him to the front door as I knew that we would get no answer there and suggested that I would go to the rear as I knew where to go. He agreed and stayed banging at the front door. I went round the back and started getting everyone out to the back yard and when everyone was out I told the owner to let the sergeant in. He gave out like hell to me for letting him at the front door. I told him that when I came round all the people were out in the back yard – which, by the way, was still part of the licensed premises, but he didn't know that – and that I got talking to them and forgot about him at the front door. Perhaps he bought my story but in any case he never took me to raid a pub again.

I got on well with all sections of the community in Ballyconnell. There were five churches in the area – Catholic, Protestant, Presbyterian, Free Presbyterian and Methodist. All the people got on well and there was never much trouble in the town. I became friendly with a few of the girls working in the only bank in the town, the Ulster Bank. One of them, a Catholic, was engaged to a fellow from Florence Court in Fermanagh – a Protestant farmer, a member of the UDR and a very nice fellow. They were having difficulty in getting a priest to attend the wedding service which was to take place in a Protestant church. I said I knew a popular priest who might attend. He used to give general absolution as he would be too busy to hear confessions and was involved in a lot of businesses including owing a coal mine as well as a number of dancehalls around the area. I approached him and he agreed to go to the wedding to represent the Catholic Church. We had a great time at the wedding and a fortnight later when the happy couple came back from honeymoon there was a party for them in Florence Court. I was on my way to this party when I was stopped by a UDR patrol (the UDR were the North's version of the FCA, but were trained and armed and on patrol). Once I said where I was going, their attitude changed completely and they were very nice to me. It was a different story at a patrol another night when I was going to the pictures in Enniskillen. They looked for identification and the only one I had on me at that time was my garda ID. The UDR man wanted to see it even though I was only the passenger in the car. I told him I would show it to him but would not give it to him. I was feeling confident and didn't like his attitude. He cocked the gun and said 'Give it to me!' 'You can kill me first and then take it,' I said. With that, fortunately, his officer came along and I explained the situation. He apologised and let us off on our way.

This party in Florence Court was great with a wide variety of people attending, including RUC, UDR, UVF, Provo and a small number of gardaí. We all got on fine and did not leave the party till daylight.

I really enjoyed my time in Ballyconnell. It was perhaps

strange that I never felt any fear in the North, yet when I returned over the border, I always felt a huge relief. Perhaps I was more nervous there than I thought.

– 4 –
Cabra

During my time in Ballyconnell my parents were not well and had to be looked after. My father suffered a stroke at work and his personality changed completely. As a young father, he was quite an unassuming man, but he became quite stubborn. I would often leave Ballyconnell at 6 a.m. after a night shift and drive home to take him into the hospital for physiotherapy. This was a good time for us to have a chat, even though that often meant me being given out to for something or other. We had our laughs too and had the same sense of humour so it was sad for me to see him going downhill and dying so young.

I applied for a transfer to Cork, even though I was quite happy where I was except for the long journey. My transfer came through eventually in 1977, not to Cork, but to Cabra in Dublin. I was now in a quandary as I felt I might never get out of Dublin but I decided to take a chance and accept the offer.

Cabra Station is on the Navan Road and it included accommodation. I was surrounded by elderly mules, mostly bachelors, who were also living-in. Cabra Station covered

Áras an Uachtaráin so most of the duty was at 'posts' (security points, where the gardaí stood at the same point for an eight-hour shift, minding the place). The older guys manned the main gates and rarely took holidays in case younger ones were put on their posts and left there. It was considered a cushy job.

My interest in racing continued and it was handy that the Phoenix Park racecourse was on our patch. I would do traffic duty and it was amazing the horse tips you would get. One day I got talking to a jockey who told me that his horse would win at the next Gowran Park meeting. The day of racing in Gowran Park it was arranged that I would go and take whatever money we had scraped together to put on the horse. Everything was set up. I was due to go down on the Thursday, with nearly £500, which in 1977 was a lot of money. I was getting the day off and we were going to make our fortune. I was awakened by one of the lads at six on the morning in question to be told that the horse was in the paper as a non-runner and that the sergeant said I was to come to work. Two weeks later I was at home in Cork listening to the sports results when the announcer called out the results from Gowran Park. Our horse had won at 8/1 and we had not a penny on it. What the jockey had told me was to back the horse the *next time he runs* at Gowran. A lesson learned to listen properly.

One thing I liked about Cabra was that it was near Dalymount Park, where Ireland used to play their matches, and also close to Croke Park. One Sunday I went to Dalymount to see Ireland play Poland, the week after they had drawn with England in Wembley and put them out of the World Cup. Their goalkeeper was Thomaseskai, known as a clown by the English. He played against us that day and we beat them one-nil; Miah Dennehy from Cork scored the winning goal. Terry Mancini, a great character, made his debut at the match. I was on duty for the All-Ireland final Cork v Wexford in 1977 and from the VIP box watched a great Cork team win the middle game in their three-in-a-row.

There were posts all around the house in Áras an Uachtaráin. The president of the time was Paddy Hillery. I found it quite confusing as he wanted us to be around, but invisible, yet when he didn't see us, he would report us to our super. I remember one Sunday morning I had been out all night and came into work and was inside in my box reading the papers and trying to sleep at the same time. At about 6.30 a.m. there was a knock on the door. I turned around and who was it, but the president himself, looking into my sleepy, blurry eyes. He asked me if I had seen his golfball. When I said I hadn't, he left and luckily did not report me.

Friday and Saturday nights were great to be on duty in Cabra, especially if you were not on a post, because there was a nightclub in the Phoenix Park and anyone who was not on a post in Áras or on car duty headed there. We also had a sergeant who used to disappear there himself, no questions asked. Clouds was a great spot and we spent many hours 'on the beat' in there.

Around teatime on my first day on duty we picked up

on a stolen car. I was in the back seat of the patrol car when the stolen car pulled in. Young Garda Jim jumps out and just as I'm approaching the driver's door of the stolen car, it drives off. The other garda quickly jumped back into the car and drove off in pursuit, leaving me on the side of the street not knowing where I was. After at least an hour and numerous calls on the radio, I established where I was and another car came and collected me. A valuable lesson – don't ever be too eager to approach stolen cars.

I was fairly small and I always said that the required height was brought down because they wanted me in the gardaí. I was the smallest in my class and also the smallest in the force at the time. The following day I was on the beat in Cabra West, me all of 5'8", my companion 6'9". I got a lot of slagging from guys who hung around the betting offices. 'Here come Little and Large ... Pigs in Space', the usual taunts, but I gained their respect when I give them a few good tips for the horses. I won the battle of wits and many of them got to know me so we would have plenty of good banter about the Dublin and Cork teams.

The Cabra area also included Dublin Zoo, located in the Phoenix Park. After the Áras, this was the next most important call for the gardaí. One night when I was in the car the alarm went off in the zoo. We arrived at the gates very fast and, as usual, I was out of the car in a flash. The animals were going ballistic so we thought there were intruders inside. I climbed up to the top of the gate so I could jump inside. However, my leg got caught in the bars so I couldn't move back or forward. The key holder arrived and coolly opened the gate next to me. They all went in and left me stranded on top of the fence. Another lesson – don't rush in.

I found Dublin a lonely place. The station party was impersonal, except for those Friday and Saturday nights in the nightclub and, even though I was living in the station with about twenty others, I never really got to know any of them. An example of that was when I went to Sofia again for another game: I met one of the lads who lived across the corridor from me in the station in Cabra. He was walking down the hallway of the Sheraton Hotel and I didn't even know he was going to be at the game.

I could not wait to get out of Dublin, so in the ten months I was there I applied five times for a transfer. Eventually I got my wish and was transferred to Mitchelstown, only twenty miles from home.

– 5 –
Mitchelstown

When I left secondary school I worked in Roches Stores and one of my supervisors was Eileen O'Brien. She was going out with Michael Murphy, and my sister Mary was going out with Michael's brother Tim; both later married their men. Eileen's sister Marian would call into the store and we would have a bit of banter. She married John Riordan and it made my day and future years to find that he was stationed in Mitchelstown and became one of my few genuine friends in the Garda Síochána.

Mitchelstown was only twenty miles from Watergrasshill so I was able to get permission to live at home with my parents and Auntie Hannah, which was a great saving. I settled in very fast as I knew a lot of people through GAA and soccer.

The station at that time was a three-storey house in Upper Cork Street. John and Marian were living there and it became a second home for me, as I would stay there with them whenever I was working late or early next morning.

Many was the great night we had in the house playing cards or Monopoly. At that time there was a man sleeping rough around the town and we all liked him. We would go down the town and bring him back to the station. The fire would be lighting and Michael (not his real name) often did SO duty, as he knew the call signs and could come in and call one of us if the phone rang. He didn't mind as he was warm and later he would go and have a sleep if the cell was vacant. We were later able to get a house for him, which he treasured and lived in until he died.

It was from one of the nights in the kitchen playing cards that the idea of doing something for the old folks came about. There was a great committee who looked after them, so our idea was to do a sponsored cycle from Mitchelstown to Glengarriff, then on to Kenmare, Killarney and back to Mitchelstown. John Riordan, Pat Mulcahy, John Sullivan and I were to ride the bikes and Marian and Martin Sheehan (now Fr Martin) were our back-up.

We left Mitchelstown at 6 a.m. on a Monday morning and our aim was to be in Glengarriff at 6 p.m., but we cycled so fast we were there earlier after spending an hour in Cork and two hours in Bantry. We got great coverage from the media, even on the nine o'clock news on RTÉ. Luckily they edited out the part where I fell off the bike on the main road in front of the cameras. The second day was over the mountains to Kenmare, which was pure torture. As I had played a tough county semi-final on the Sunday prior to the cycle, I was still stiff and sore. I was really struggling when a car started beeping behind me. I waved it on, but when it passed me the driver held a £10 note out the window. I cycled fast to get the money and it got me over that mountain. We got a great reception wherever we went, particularly back in Mitchelstown on the Thursday, which was market day in the town. We collected over £2,500 which went towards the building of the old folk's houses.

While I was stationed in Mitchelstown my mother was diagnosed with breast cancer and had a breast removed. At the same time her memory was going due to secondaries in her brain and spine; in a way it was a godsend as she could not remember how severe her chemotherapy was. At that time my brother Eamon's wife Pat had twins, Des and Jackie, and they all lived across the road from my parents' house in the village. Each day my mother would take the twins for a walk in the double buggy with their brother Don and sister Michelle.

My father was also pretty sick and had taken to the bed. One Sunday morning, I tried to get him up for mass but he refused, saying, 'I will probably be dead when you get back.' I said, 'If you are you can stay there as Cork is playing Kerry in a league final in the Mardyke.' Lo and behold when I got back from mass he was up and ready, waiting to be taken to the match. I told him there was no seating there, but he said he would stand and would have no problem walking down to the venue. The Mardyke is a long walk from the Mercy Hospital, but he walked every inch of it and stood for the hour the match was playing. Where there's a will, there's a way.

The Mitchelstown sub-district was notorious for acci-

Left to right: John O'Sullivan, Pat Mulcahy, Paddy O'Callaghan, myself and John Riordan

dents, particularly on the main Dublin to Cork road. When these accidents happened on the main road a lot of them were fatal, which was hard on us gardaí as we had no training for dealing with emotions, our own or others', so we had to deal with them as best we could.

My first fatal accident was at the pedestrian lights in the middle of the town, in which an eight-year-old girl was mown down by a drunken driver. The driver hit her on the crossing but then drove away and around the town. He then parked below the crossing to make it look like the child ran out in front of his car. All my witnesses were seven- and eight-year-olds who had been with the girl.

What made the situation even harder to deal with was that the child was the daughter of a colleague of mine. I didn't know it at the time and wanted to charge the driver with manslaughter as I felt we might not get a plea of dangerous driving causing death. However, this was not acceptable to the powers that be as there wasn't sufficient evidence, so he was only charged with drunken driving and dangerous driving. The result was that he got off the dangerous driving charge and was only put off the road for drunken driving.

The Garda Síochána do not train you to deal with death. You have to learn as you go along. I had to deal with a lot: sudden, suicide and murder. I always found it hard to handle, but I think the one I found most difficult to deal with was a cot death. The child was asleep in its cot in the back of the car, the mother checked the child to see if it was o.k. and a few minutes later, when she checked again, to her horror her beautiful baby was taken from her, unexplained, no reason. Trying to deal with that on a Sunday evening, trying to find the right words and do your job at the same time was close to impossible. Even twenty-five years on, as I write these words, I am still affected by it.

One day I was on the phone dealing with some press people about a pollution spillage into the local river when I heard Mick Burke on town patrol whispering into the radio that there was a bank raid on the Allied Irish Bank. I had the misfortune to say to the reporter that I had to go as there was a bank robbery taking place. I mobilised as many gardaí as I could to go down to the scene. The news spread like wildfire and the phones in the station kept ringing – RTÉ, *Echo*, *Examiner*, *Times*, *Independent*, *Press* – I was up the walls! The raiders held Mick at gunpoint and kept the two gardaí, sergeants Towey and O'Keeffe, at bay and made their escape. A big chase and search ensued all around the Ballyduff area of West Waterford. Two of the culprits were arrested but the money was never recovered. The funny thing was that the Thursday before that, information had come through that the Bank of Ireland in Baldwin Street was to be raided. The town was saturated with gardaí so nothing had happened until the following week.

One of the great occasions in this country was the visit of Pope John Paul II to Ireland. All garda leave was cancelled and personnel were sent all over the country. We were detailed to go to the youth mass in Galway and so we left from Mallow railway station on the Saturday and headed for Galway. There was a great buzz in the country and none more so than in Galway. We were all detailed for our duties and headed down to the racecourse. All areas were sectioned off so that there would be no crushing. There was great atmosphere and craic on that day. How ironic it is now to see clips of the Galway visit – the two priests keeping the crowd entertained were Bishop Eamonn Casey and Fr Michael Cleary. We had been standing and walking all night, and at one stage John Riordan and I found a nice quiet corner behind a tent and decided to have a sit down. We left Galway at 2 a.m. that Monday night and arrived back in Mitchelstown around 7 a.m. – a long time to be on your feet, without sleep. It was a great success, without incident, and it was great to have played a small part in it.

As there was no town council in Mitchelstown, there were no town by-laws, so you could not give a ticket to anyone for double-parking. This was a big problem as people would abandon their cars and go shopping. If you wanted to prosecute a driver, you had to wait for them to come back to their cars and get their name and address, then make out a summons for them to go to court. More often than not these cases were not heard and thrown out of court. One such day I was on the town beat when I saw a car double-parked on Upper Cork Street. I met the driver, an elderly man who I knew to see, and told him that he was to move his car. He did this, but only as far as the next shop. He then repeated this action, double-parking all the way down the town. Eventually I threatened to summons him and he got the message.

One Sunday evening we had a traffic accident just outside the town on the main road at the Cork side of Mitchelstown. Two cars were involved, a married couple and five youths from the travelling community. When I arrived all seven were injured so I needed to get two or three ambulances. Mitchelstown is thirty miles from Cork, thirty miles from Cashel, twenty miles from Mallow and ten miles from Fermoy, where the nearest ambulances are based. After a long wait they arrived and all the injured were taken away from the scene. Squad cars accompanied the ambulances and I got word back that they had to stop up the road as one of the youths had almost died, but they managed to get him breathing again. Another report was that another one had died, but he also recovered. They were all taken to Cork Regional Hospital (now Cork University Hospital). I had no names or addresses for the youths as they were not able to answer me, so bad were their injuries. Having finished my work at the scene, I enquired from the hospital how the injured were and I was informed that the five youths had disappeared from the hospital, never to be seen again. I call it the 'Miracle on Cork Road'. The couple had no re-dress for compensation except from the Motor Bureau of Ireland and that takes a long time, but I think they did finally receive it.

Once I arrived in Mitchelstown, my sporting travels really took off and I was able to get to all hurling, football and soccer matches. I was in a position to get block bookings for all the away matches as I had established connections with people involved in soccer.

Copenhagen was our next port of call for the 3–3 European game in May 1978. This was a lovely trip as when we crossed over on the ferry we also got a chance to visit Malmo in Sweden. My abiding memory of Malmo was the cleanness of the streets and the high price of shoes: men's shoes cost the equivalent of €120 a pair. I was glad we had good old St Bernard's of Dunnes Stores at home. We also played Belgium, England and Northern Ireland in that group. The trip to Wembley was followed by a visit to Highbury and we managed to get on the pitch and have an imaginary penalty shoot-out, without a ball. Innocent days.

During this era Argentina, the world champions, came to play in Dublin and the very young Maradona came on in that game. Even at this stage we could see he was going to be a special talent. The match was on during a petrol strike but we had managed to secure petrol in cans and bottles. On the way up to the match, we hid our stash of petrol in a ditch for the return journey. As it happened, we found a petrol station open with no queue and we filled up the car there, picked up our cans and bottles and brought them back to Cork to keep for future needs.

After the match in Wembley huge crowds were trying to get on the Underground train so we decided to get on one going in the opposite direction to most of the crowd. We ended up in the National Ballroom where, in the toilet, a young fellow came up to me and said 'how's it going?' It turned out he remembered me from my duties in Mitchelstown. He went on to remind me about an incident outside the Mayflower Ballroom. It was a Saturday night when I was station orderley and I got a call from the owner of the ballroom saying there was a big crowd of young fellows with iron bars trying to get into the ballroom. I called the squad car again and again but got no reply, so I decided to go up in my own car.

On arrival I saw about twenty youths so I had to devise a plan to try to stay alive. I got out of the car and banged the door again and again as if there were a few of us and shouted, 'Up against the wall the whole f...ing lot of ye!' With that they all turned and faced the wall. What next? I was on my own, a small guard against twenty of them with their hands against the wall! I started searching the line at one end and one fellow dropped an iron bar. Once the others heard the heavy sharp sound, the others dropped theirs. This was a fine collection of weapons as there would be a fight every Saturday night between Fermoy, Cahir and Mitchelstown. There were gangs of youths intent on mischief who caused a lot of trouble so we were always busy. Eventually help arrived before they realised I was alone.

Another night I was SO and there was a knock on the door of the station. In front of me were four youths from Fermoy, aged about seventeen, who said they had been stabbed by guys from Cahir. They had received serious wounds. I called the patrol car but got no reply as there were several black spots in the area for reception. I called for a doctor and ambulance, getting a barrage of abuse from the four, one of them going in and out of consciousness. Next came another knock at the door, this time four youths from Cahir who told me they had been stabbed by the Fermoy guys. They came in and all hell broke loose in the station, with them flicking blood from their own wounds at one another. Eventually I restored order but, unbeknowns to me, both gangs made a pact not to tell me anything. The situation was compounded when the doctor, a locum, arrived, he himself full to the brim with drink and hardly able to talk. My main concern was for one of the Fermoy boys who had been stabbed in the stomach and backside. I was worried he was going to die, but thankfully an ambulance arrived and all survived.

Another night I was SO having a nice peaceful tour of duty, when Mossie Joyce, a security officer in Mitchelstown Creameries, arrived in the station and told me there was a big fight downtown and that my colleagues, John Riordan and Pat Fletcher, needed help. I put on my tunic and cap and headed down to Lower Cork Street to find John and Pat in big trouble, both their shirts torn from their backs. The street was blocked with ten to fifteen members of the travelling community, two gardaí – John and Pat – and a big crowd of onlookers. I was the only one looking like a garda at that stage and was met with a huge haymaker of a punch and put flying. I soon forgot the oath I took when I joined the gardaí – 'without fear, fervour or ill will' – and with a little help from onlookers we restored order to our satisfaction. Ten of the travellers were sent off to hospital for treatment and later brought before the courts and received sentences. I never did get to the bottom of how the fight started.

A new garda station was promised in Mitchelstown for many years and eventually it arrived. I happened to be the last SO in the old station and the first in the new station. At the time it was thought we might get disturbance money as the ESB and others had done but, as we only had to move two doors away, we had no such luck. It was a fine new station with three cells and plenty of space and a kitchen which was never used.

At that time whoever was on car patrol would go for his break either to the security man in the creamery or to the security man in the co-op. One particular Friday night, the lads went to the co-op and while they were having their tea they heard a noise in the shop. On investigating, they found a twenty-five-year-old man in the shop. He had hidden himself there until after closing. He was arrested and brought to the station. He was from Cork city so we placed him in a cell until the morning when he would be charged. I was SO overnight and in the morning when my relief arrived I went downtown for breakfast. When I came back, I was told that our friend had escaped, hijacked a car and was heading towards Glanworth. Some of the gardaí followed him and I got into my car and went out the Mallow road.

I spotted him in the passenger seat of a car, turned my car around and followed him to the square in the town, where he got out. I roared at him to stop but he took off, racing like a hare. I and my eighteen stone seemed no match for him but, despite slipping, momentum spurred by a large burst of adrenaline saw me up a lane after him. He jumped over a gate, I got hold of his leg, but one hand was not enough to hold him and I had to let him go. I noticed a small door in the gate and bust it open to be met by a concrete block heading towards my head. Luckily enough I saw it at the last second, ducked, and caught my man on the ground.

At this stage a number of people had gathered and I asked someone to help me or get help. With that he turned on me, kicked me in the head and took off. He disappeared, but after a few hours we found him hiding in a backyard shed not far away. He was brought to the station and charged; after a court case he got a few years in jail. Shortly afterwards I was in Shannon Airport and there he was walking towards me. He passed me by and laughed in my face. I later enquired why he was out of jail and was told that he had appealed his sentence and it was not contested. I was never told about the appeal but I later found out that he was very well known within the army circles and had as much influence as he needed. I wonder how far his influence would have got him if that concrete block had killed or maimed me.

Another incident in the co-op illustrates that you should never, ever, change your mind: one day I got a phonecall from the co-op about a shoplifter who had taken a valuable coat. Security were following the culprit and I met up with them on Upper John Street. When we caught up to the man he said he had bought the coat elsewhere and was wearing it when he went into the store. The co-op had had only one of these coats and it was now gone but the security guys started to have doubts about what they had really seen. Eventually we had to allow him to go with the coat. He then turned around and sued the co-op for false arrest and they had to pay up. So he got a new coat and expenses for coming to Mitchelstown to steal the coat.

There were not many domestic disputes in Mitchelstown, but I will always remember Mary and Jack Murphy (not their real names) who were always fighting, so much so that the Health Board took their children from them. They both had drink problems. On one summer's day Mary called to the station and said that Jack had locked her out of the house and could we go with her to try and get her back into the house. John Riordan and I went with her and found that the doors were locked. We called Jack but all he would do was abuse us and tell us to eff off. John spotted a window that could be opened enough to get his hand in to open the door. We asked Mary if it was ok to do this and she said 'of course'. John went up onto the window-sill and got the door open. Mary walked in, followed by us, but she then turned and asked us where we were going. We replied that we wanted to talk to Jack but she told us that we couldn't come in without a warrant and banged the door in our faces. After that, we were slow to offer assistance to her.

One of the worst duties at Mitchelstown were cordon points. These were the checkpoints established on all the bridges in north Cork when some event like a kidnapping or bank robbery happened. Our cordon point was Ballyhooly Bridge – as cold a spot as you would find anywhere in Ireland. You could find yourself on this bridge for up to twelve hours with no relief. I was there one night in the middle of winter and to keep warm and not to fall asleep I started walking over and back on the bridge. In the still of the night I heard a car a long way away. I don't know what grabbed my attention about this car but I could hear it getting nearer. As I started walking back across the bridge towards my car, the other car came down the slip road and onto the bridge. I raised my hand for the car to stop but it kept coming towards me. I had to jump out of the way and onto the bridge, aware that I could not swim and did not want to die in the water in Ballyhooly. I clung on and, lucky for me, the car kept going. I got down from the bridge and into my own car and followed. On a corner about 100 yards away, out in the middle of the road, was the car with no-one in it. The boys had vanished from the car which had been stolen in Fermoy.

– 6 –

Moving On

I always had a great interest in music, no matter what it was, as long as it was good. From Elvis to Cliff to the Beatles, Status Quo, the Rolling Stones, Charlie Pride, Rod Stewart, forty years later they are all still in demand. Popular Irish showbands were Brendan Boyer and the Royal, Brendan O'Brien, Joe Mac and the Dixies, Dickie Rock, the original Miami, Butch Moore and the Capital, and who could forget Derek Deane, Billy Browne and the Freshmen. The likes of Big Tom, Daniel O'Donnell, Margo and Brendan Shine all had large followings too. In the Cork area the choice of venues was brilliant as there were at least thirty ballrooms such as the Majorca, Crosshaven; Majestic, Mallow; Pinewood, Glenville; Mayflower, Mitchelstown; Top Hat, Fermoy; and the Lilac, Enniskeane. It's a pity that all of these are now closed. During the 1960s and 1970s dancing was huge in Ireland. In the height of the showband boom, there were about 800 showbands in the country.

One of the real favourite ballrooms in Cork was the Arcadia, on the Lower Glanmire Road, where there was dancing about four nights a week. Wednesday night was called Dinosaurs and was mainly for students, promoted by a group of students at UCC including Robin Power, who went on to head Power Securities. Recently the Arcadia was knocked and apartment blocks built in its place. I would have thought the city council would have put a preservation order on the outside of it as it had a very distinctive outer wall and holds memories of great nights for thousands of Cork dancers. It was also the first building people saw when they arrived in Cork by train.

This was an era when there were no bars in the dancehalls and people often went dancing five or six nights a week to all the different venues. I always had a grá for Irish groups such as Cry Before Dawn, Thin Lizzy, Aslan, Horslips, the Boomtown Rats, Something Happens, the Blades, and Mama's Boys. The McManus Brothers came from Derrylin in Co. Fermanagh and I remember talking to them as small boys in the back of their parents' car as they were great musicians. Later came the Stunning, and a great band from Sligo called Those Nervous Animals, along with our own Cork bands the Sultan of Ping and the Frank and Walters (who I got to play one night at a party in the Garda Club – they were awesome). They were great bands who could have made it to the top internationally but it was U2, the Cranberries and the Corrs who got the luck.

One of my favourite Cork bands was called Double Vision; I got to know them very well and often travelled with them to gigs. In fact, when my son, Brendan, was small he wanted to be a crew member and we set it up one night and decked him out in a t-shirt. Off he went in the van and helped to set up and later replace the gear into the van. He got a great kick out of it, and so did I.

I knew Double Vision were good but it was only lately when I saw a video of them that was made over fifteen years ago that I realised how great they were. They had an amazing lead singer in Kieran Kramer and the best box player I have seen in Pat Sullivan – a magnificent musician, still playing. When he got the box out and started playing the whole place rocked. When they broke up they all went different ways – some formed the group Bog the Donkey who are still going strong. I don't know how they do it; it looks a glamorous life but it's pretty tough and tiring.

I remember going to one Double Vision gig with them: I was picked up in Cork at 3.30 p.m. on the Saturday and we drove to Claremorris in Mayo, had something to eat, then continued on to Crossmalina for the gig. Once there, the van had to be emptied and the gear set up and sound-checked. They started playing at 11.30 p.m. with no-one in hall and at 12.30, after the pubs closed, the hall started to fill up. The gig ended at 2.30 a.m., but they took time to talk to fans before taking down gear and getting it back in the van. At 4.30 a.m. we left Crossmalina and arrived back in Cork at midday. They started the whole process again later that day and went to another venue that night for more of the same.

Sunday night was a Macra night and attracted people from all around the countryside. One or two of the lads met a woman, or as we'd say, 'shifted', and then headed back to the car to go home. There were seven in the car, so one particular girl had nowhere else to sit but on my knee. This was the start of my courtship with Catherine Foley who was later to become Catherine Ryan.

We got married on 25 July 1980 and moved in with Auntie Hannah. My parents had died at this stage. Our only child, Brendan, was born ten months later. I was present at the birth which was frightening and exciting all in one. He was a small little fellow and I had to go out and buy a hat for him as he had a tender head. His mother and I went to a film in Cork the day before he was born. These days he is addicted to films.

Brendan is now a garda, having graduated on 24 July 2006. He got an early education in the workings of the Garda Síochána. One Sunday while I was stationed in Mitchelstown, I was in the car and was also minding Brendan, who was three or four years of age at the time. He came in the patrol car with me and was having a great time in the Ne-Naw car, standing between the seats; there were no compulsory seatbelts in those days. I was then sent a message that there was a dispute over a right of way, so we headed off to the location. On arrival I was met by a man who told me that there had been a shot fired in the incident. As I walked up the avenue holding Brendan in my arms, I met the parties involved and came to the conclusion that if I could get rid of the wife of one of the parties we would make progress, so I handed her Brendan and asked her to take him inside to mind him for me. It worked and we sorted out the problem to everyone's satis-

Brendan on his passing out in 2006 with his mum, Catherine, and myself; (inset) at age four

faction. That was Brendan's first bit of garda duty.

Mitchelstown was a great town with lovely people and a great station 'party' – we always refer to staff as a party. I loved it there. We had a number of haunts or, as I call them, 'safe houses'. Whenever I was on town patrol, my first port of call was Geary's pub: in the back door to be greeted by a number of friends, all drinking coffee, before hours. Then I would go across the road to the Torten coffee shop for another chat. It was there one morning that I met a friend I had worked with in Roches Stores, but had kept up contact with; Liam O'Brien was a very funny man and great craic. This morning I had brand new handcuffs and Liam was very interested in them. I demonstrated on him by handcuffing him to the stool he was sitting on. Unfortunately I discovered that I had no keys, so I had to leave him there, handcuffed to the stool for an hour. He found it highly amusing, but didn't ask to see my handcuffs again.

As there was no election on the horizon, the new station in Mitchelstown was never officially opened. We decided that instead we would have a dinner dance with a reception in the station beforehand. At the time we were limited to 120 people in the Clongibbon Hotel. We decided that the reception in the station would start at 7 p.m. with punch, followed by finger food. We sold the 120 tickets and set about getting the station ready. We decided to make the punch ourselves so one of the lads got a recipe and early that morning we began demonstrating our culinary skills. We had sussed out some poteen from west Clare, and got wine and any other concoction that we could find. We got a Burco boiler and added the ingredients plus a bag of fruit and turned the boiler on to slow to let it marinate gently for the day. That evening when everyone sampled the punch they thought it was lovely and smooth. The evening progressed nicely and when everyone left to head for the hotel, they hit the fresh air and became very 'happy'. The following year we had to celebrate the opening of the station again, but this time something like 300 people wanted to attend.

I was always amused at how people made up their minds on a situation involving a garda, and it always seemed that the prisoner was really the victim and we were the criminals. Typically, one night John Riordan and I were on duty in the patrol car. There was a dance on in the Mayflower ballroom, so we went in for a look, as we always did, just to show we were around. We left the car parked up the street a little bit and as we were leaving we saw two guys fighting, so we separated them. We knew one of them well, but we hadn't seen the other before. When we asked him his name he got aggressive and head-butted me. I arrested him for assault; the other guy walked away.

As we were taking the prisoner up the street to the patrol car, people started coming onto the street from the dance-hall. The prisoner saw these people and started a rumpus, shouting and roaring. With that a few people came over to us and tried to take the prisoner away. The crowd got bigger and angrier and soon we were surrounded by people. But we were not going to let our man go, no way! We edged our way slowly towards the car, being hit and punched all the time. People were getting involved and didn't even know why or what was going on. We eventually got into the car but it was lifted off the ground and the mob tried to turn it over. At this stage we were in fear of our lives as we didn't know what they were going to do next.

Then at the door of the car appeared the guy who was in the original fight and asked 'Jim, do you want me to come to the station, as well?' I politely told him where to go. John started the car and eventually we got away. A typical case of people getting involved in something they knew nothing about and taking sides against the gardaí.

Another night I was SO in the station at a time when there were threats that the UVF were going to try to bomb Cork. I was sitting in the station when I got a phonecall from an operator that he had received a message from a male caller to say there was a bomb in the Firgrove Hotel. I knew they were holding a dance there that night and I also knew it was a hoax, but I could not take a chance. The car was too far away so I decided to go to the hotel myself. With over 1,000 people in the venue I decided on a strategy to avoid a panic situation. I got all the bouncers and staff together, told them to open all the doors and by individual word of mouth to get people to leave. When most of the people were outside we got the band to stop playing. As usual, a few people would not leave and I had my suspicions that it was one of them who had made the phonecall. We searched the whole place and of course found nothing, but it was a cheap, mean and nasty thing to do.

One night I was on car patrol again, bored, so I met one of the lads who was off-duty that night. I really wanted to go to the dance in the Mayflower to hear the band so he said he would work for me instead. We went into the dressing room where the band was getting ready and changed into each other's clothes with the guys in the band looking at us, a garda and a civilian. We don't know what they made of us but I went off dancing and my friend left in my uniform to do my work in the patrol car.

During my time in the gardaí I had a number of supers and they all had their own little quirks: Jim Brogan in Ballyconnell, liked to play pool. My super in Dublin (I saw him only once) was known as Nugget Head as it was thought he put polish on his bald head. My first super in Mitchelstown was John Finlay, a Dubliner, who was rarely around and who headed back to Dublin any chance he got. Then came Sean Murray, an ex-army man who valued cleanliness and had a military way about him. I always got on well with Seamus O'Hanlon when he arrived in Fermoy district headquarters. Seamus was the man who, on being presented with a gift on his transfer back up to Monaghan, said the only one he saw working in Fermoy station was the cleaning lady.

I was in the Torten one morning at 10.15 when I got a call from the station. Gerry Quinn was the SO that morning and called me over the radio for my location. I had left the station at approx 9.45, and I replied, 'where do you think I am?' 'Clonmel, is it?' he said, so I knew that Seamus Kerins, my new super, must have been within earshot; he and I didn't like each other very much. I ran out the back door, across some alleys and down into the square, where I stopped a friend, Mossie Joyce, and asked him to go to the station and see if the super's car was outside the station. A mobile phone would have been handy then. Mossie came back and told me where his car was situated, so I was able to get closer and have a look. I spotted the super crossing the road, getting into his car and heading towards me. I started turning so that when he passed me I would have my back to him and would be able to pretend I didn't know he was around. It seemed to work at the time as he never stopped to talk to me but he had his revenge on me later: one morning, out of the blue, while I was SO, a D20 notice of transfer came. I had not applied for it, didn't want it, but I was going to Cork City ten years after I had applied for it. All of a sudden, so it seems, I was badly needed in the city. The super had decided to get me out of his sight.

– 7 –

The Independent Republic of Watercourse Road

I appealed my transfer: first to the super, but as he wanted rid of me he was not going to go against himself; then to the chief super, but he wouldn't go against the super, and neither would the commissioner. All that was left was what was called a 'review body'. This was made up of three people: a member of my union, the Garda Representative Association (GRA); a commissioner; and a Department of Justice representative. I went to the meeting in Dublin with my GRA representative, Mick McNamara, who explained that it would be two to one whichever way the decision went. Inside the room the three were sitting at a desk with a file, I presume, on me. I didn't know what I was defending myself against as I had no access to the file or what was said about me. If I were a mass murderer I would have access to the Book of Evidence and could properly defend myself. To this day, I have never been told why I was transferred; I would like to believe that it was because Cork City needed me but I don't think so seeing that my replacement knew he was coming to Mitchelstown before I knew I was being shafted. I considered taking a case to the High Court as I felt it was totally unconstitutional, as I still do, but was advised against it by my solicitor, who probably felt I could not afford to take the case. I still think I would have won my case as there wasn't any particular reason for my transfer; I didn't look for it and wasn't consulted about it. We will never know.

Eventually I arrived in Watercourse Road station in Cork and was met by the station IC, a wonderful man called Donie Sullivan. The station at that time was a temporary one over the 147 Snooker Club. Donie had led the lads on a walkout of the rat-infested building next door where the station had originally been located and where the new station currently is. I vaguely knew Donie as he had been a garda in Rathcormac, just down the road from Watergrasshill, and had played hurling with Bride Rovers. I told him openly that I had not wanted to come to that station, nothing against him, but I was not a happy camper. I was looking on the posting as semi-retirement. He said he understood and that we would see how things went.

As it happened, I soon got into the swing of things in Watercourse Road. There was a great family feeling amongst the station party; we used to call it the Independent Republic of Watercourse Road. It was a really happy place with some great characters and very honourable guys, good policemen who were wise and not appreciated outside of Watercourse Road. It was, for some reason, considered a punishment to be sent to this station, so we all got on really well together. The teabreaks both morning and evening were sacred and everybody tried to make them. I had been off the cigarettes before I arrived but I soon found I needed to smoke if I wanted to fit in. Lots of the gardaí from around the city and county would call in if they wanted to know something or other. We had a good network of gardaí with useful information so Watercourse Road was the place to go.

Mick Kelly, one of the lads in Watercourse Road, had been stationed in Fermoy while I was in Mitchelstown. He was a genius and had no problem taking on authority. Anyone who had a problem would call to Mick; most supers were afraid of him. If he had put his mind to it he could have been commissioner but he preferred to remain a 'pleb' like the rest of us. An out and out Fíanna Fáil man, he christened the PD Party 'Pricks and Deserters'. Mick got cancer and died in early June 1988 and is buried in his native Cobh. I missed his funeral as I had arranged leave to go on a special trip to Germany for Euro '88 and I needed to head off that day. I knew he would understand.

Also in the office at that stage was John Harrington, a native of the Béara peninsula, and Kathleen Ryan (no relation to me), the civilian clerk who had an address in County Cork but for some reason claimed she was from Kerry, which caused great banter. Donie O'Sullivan was our boss. He ran a great station and was very well respected.

I had no fear in the city and would walk anywhere without thinking about trouble; I always thought I could talk my way out of any situation. One night after closing time I went into one of Blackpool's tougher pubs to get them to lock up but was completely ignored. I eventually got the drinkers out but not without a lot of remarks suggesting it would be more in my line to be doing real garda work and catching real criminals – you will always get that when you catch someone doing something illegal. As I was leaving I told everyone that I would be back the next night at 12.15 a.m. and expected them to be gone. My motivation was to get everyone out, the pub closed, and people off the street so we could have a hassle-free night. That was the plan.

True to my word, at 12.15 the next night, in the door I went and got them all to get out, leaving their drinks behind them. I told them I would be back the next night at 12.01 a.m. – closing time was 11.30 – so all out at 12 midnight. The next night I arrived at a minute past twelve and made them all leave their drinks after them. My message got across and I think after that they respected me for taking them on. I never had trouble from that pub and in fact the customers there would always salute me afterwards.

I regularly read the death notices and some of my friends called me Follow-the-Coffin as I went to so many funerals. My study of the death notices came in handy one day when an elderly woman came into the station distressed. She had bought a handbag in a charity shop, but in it found over £2,000 sterling. She assumed it was drug money. I looked at the bag and found a name which corresponded to one I remembered seeing in the deaths column of the *Cork Examiner* a few weeks earlier. I eventually made contact with the relatives. They had cleared the house after the funeral but had not checked inside the bag and were delighted to find the extra money.

When we were on nights, we always had places to go for a cuppa when things died down. One such place was a garage on the Lower Road, where all sorts – taxi drivers, lorry drivers, guards – gathered for a chat and a bit of banter. We all mixed well. Two men worked there: Christy on weeknights and Hairy Christy on weekends. It was the safest and most patrolled premises in Cork. We would get a cup of tea for free, but everything else had to be paid for. Gardaí would come from different parts of the city as it was one of the few garages open all night at that stage. There was never a problem there as the 'gougers' knew it was a gardaí watering hole. When the garage closed we found a new haunt for our evening cuppa. We would all gather and talk to Peter O'Leary who worked there. He was a young fellow and everyone liked him. The same protocol was observed – free tea, everything else paid for. Customers never drove off without paying because they knew a garda might show up. It was cheap security. When Peter left, the new man refused to leave any gardaí in so we stopped calling. From that night on there was a huge amount of drive-offs. We then found a new haunt, which as far as I know is still going.

We prevented at least one suicide one night when we spotted a woman who was about to drive into the Lee in her car. We got her keys and persuaded her to go and stay with a friend, who turned out to be pregnant, for the night. After an hour, sitting and making sure she was settled in, the friend went into labour. We called an ambulance and put our suicidal woman in charge of operations. Distracted and with a purpose, she found more to think of than herself and it seemed to change her thinking on life. As far we know she is still alive. That night we saved one from leaving and helped another into the world. Score: 2–0.

Blackpool Village in Cork City is built on the River Bride which flows through and enters the River Lee near Cork Opera House. The tide is often high enough for a little water to come out onto the street near Blackpool church. In November 2002 however, in the middle of the night the Bride burst its banks and flooded most of William O'Brien Street, at the back of Blackpool church. A few weeks later it happened again: I was on duty early one Friday morning preserving a scene for examination at the end of Watercourse Road. A few motorists stopped and told me that water was coming out onto the street. Once the examination was completed I left the scene and headed up Watercourse Road. As I came up towards Blackpool around 8 a.m., I could see the water coming down the street against me. I immediately requested sandbags and help from the army. At this stage the water had come some 200 yards down the street. Quite a number of people were trapped in their homes but were in no danger. We did all in our power to help people and tried to reassure them that things would be okay, but it must have been difficult for them to stand back and see their property being destroyed.

Eventually an army lorry arrived with an army officer looking spic and span. I was wet through at this stage and the officer refused to acknowledge me, asking instead for the sergeant, who was not available. I told him this and that I was the garda in charge. He got out of the lorry and walked away. The driver and I went off down through the flood, making our way into Corcoran's Quay where people were confined but not panicking. The water finally subsided at about 11 a.m. and it was only then that anyone above the rank of garda appeared on the scene. They all arrived in their nice clean uniforms and shoes while those of us on the scene were soaked to the skin with mud and water. The whole area around the church was destroyed and carpets and furniture that had been replaced from the first flood had to be replaced again. The cause of the problem was a culvert under the road blocked with barrels, washing machines, bicycles and bits of old cars, so when the water rose it had nowhere to go but out onto the street. This has since been rectified.

There were many famous people at the time in Blackpool. In sport, if you didn't have county medals or All-Irelands you weren't worth knowing: Jack Lynch, Christy Ring, Josie Hartnett, John Lyons and Tomás Mulcahy all played with the Glen Rovers team. Joe Lynch, Niall Tobin, Donal Farmer, Liam Heffernan and the brand new hero, Jonathan Rhys-Myers, who I knew when he was a young fellow coming into the 147 Snooker Hall next door to the station, are amongst the many famous people you would meet most days in Blackpool.

– 8 –

Community Policing

After about two years in Watercourse Road, I was offered the job of 'community garda', a new concept in policing which assigned a garda to a particular area. I jumped at the opportunity as I had always considered myself a people person. My area was Farranree and its environs, which was great as I already knew a lot of people and those I didn't, knew who I was. Eamon, my brother, had also just trained Na Piarsaig, based in Farranree, to their first ever senior hurling county.

One of the first things I tried to do was to set up a group of all those working for the area, as I felt we were all doing basically the same work, but separately. We met every Monday morning for coffee in the convent in Farranree. In the group were the parish sister, a curate, a youth worker, home school links teachers and a school attendance officer. We got on well and had a system where a different one of us chaired each meeting. We identified areas we thought needed to be worked on and tackled different jobs. As a group, we were more successful than the local representatives and none of us were even looking for votes.

Donie O'Sullivan and myself outside Farranree Community Centre

One example of our work was in an overgrown area known as Pophams Field which was a haven for drug dealers. We approached the corporation to get the field flattened and made into a nice park for all the people in the area to enjoy. We also had a look at the street lighting which we managed to have upgraded.

I opened a sub-station of my own in the community centre where people could come and meet me to talk or to get forms signed. There was an official opening and a great crowd attended, although no politician or senior garda turned up except for my sergeant, Donie O'Sullivan. He saw the value of bringing a service to the people instead of expecting them to walk to Watercourse Road station to get passports and other forms signed. I would be there every Tuesday, even when I was not detailed for duty. It went really well and the people of the area appreciated the service so much that I decided to extend the service to the top of Farranree, where I had the use of an office at the rear of the church.

Among my duties was to visit the schools in the area, which I did on a regular basis. I would try and visit each class at least once a term. There were fifteen schools including the North Monastery, St Vincent's, Farranferris and the schools in Farranree. I would insist on the kids calling me Jim or Garda Jim, and not any of the other names I called out like Pig, Bluebottle, etc. They got a great kick out of my knowing all the names they had for gardaí. I always got a great reception in the schools and to this day I meet people who call me Garda Jim and wonder if I remember them from their classes.

One of the downsides of these visits was that all the schools were run by nuns, priests and brothers and they all expected me to eat with them. One day I remember having a dinner at 12.30 in the North Mon, arriving in Farranferris at 2 p.m. and having to eat another dinner, then being invited to the convent in Farranree for high tea at 5 p.m. No wonder I put on weight.

In 1989, we moved into our new station at Watercourse Road. The day of the opening I was allowed to invite seven guests, so I decided to invite children from the various schools. It's interesting to note that of the seven, one is now a model, another a soccer international, one a basketball international and others successful in business. Also in a picture taken on that day is someone who has since done time – the man who opened the station, and the Minister for Justice – Ray Burke.

I was not a great believer in Neighbourhood Watch, as I felt it only paid lip-service to the politicians who would demand figures for their Dáil questions. To me, it was an excuse to avoid supplying the necessary number of gardaí to the area. In any case, my experience was that the person nominated, or who nominated themselves as co-ordi-

Myself and Brendan with the lord mayor, Micheál Martin, and Bishop Buckley who visited the summer camp in Farranree

nator, was usually the least liked in an area and no-one would tell them anything of any use anyway, so nothing really happened and the purpose was defeated.

Our community group's plan was to try and get each street and road to organise their own residence groups and to help them to have pride in their own place. We arranged a public meeting and 500 people turned up. Everyone was in agreement that they would give it a go. That is, until the henchman of a politician in the area got into his stride and lambasted us. How he did this is hard to put into words but what I know is that before long the meeting was in uproar and our dream was gone. I don't know what the politician's agenda was. Perhaps as it was not his idea in the first place he decided to put our idea to bed, just in case it did work.

We continued to work away as a group, sharing our ideas and knowledge, but found that there was a small lobby of people, who were not involved, who were trying to undermine anything we tried to do. Perhaps in their eyes we were too powerful, I don't know.

In November 1992, while still on community policing, I sent in a submission to my super entitled: Child/Sex Abuse. It said:

> As a community guard, I feel that there are two big social problems in this country, one being the drugs problem and the other is child/sex abuse. I feel that there seems to be ignorance on everyone's part in relation to the very increasing amount of child abuse. As a police force I feel we do not

At the opening of the new station in Watercourse Road; I'm second from the right in the middle row.

> seem to know enough about this problem i.e. tell-tale signs, etc. I would like to suggest that each member of the force, both male and female, would be able to do a course on this problem, so that all of us would have knowledge of same. Forward up the line for observation please.

Three weeks later I was taken off community policing and reverted to ordinary duties. People in the area were keen to have me stay and I didn't want to go. A committee was set up and a campaign started to keep me. It got as far as a question being asked in the Dáil but no satisfactory answer was given except that it was an internal matter and that it was not disciplinary. The ironic thing was that no one wanted the job and they found it very hard to fill the vacancy.

Later on a similar job came up and I was the only one who applied for it, so it was advertised again, and this time someone else applied. I pulled out the day before the interviews, telling the super that if I couldn't get the job when I was the only applicant, I would hardly get it when they had put someone up against me.

While back on ordinary duty, it bugged me that I had never got a reply to my original query so, after a number of enquiries in March 1993, I got the following reply from a senior officer of the Garda Síochána:

> I have noted the report re. Child Sexual Abuse by Garda Ryan. I take the view that much of the child abuse hysteria is part of a concentrated plan by certain interests to promote

> so-called 'Sex Education' in schools. Contrary to what has been claimed child abuse is not as prevalent as some would have us believe – it is as low as one in 300 children. Therefore to suggest that the gardaí should get involved in some special measurement/programmes which include drenching innocent schoolchildren in sex information is to repeat the mistakes already made in the U.S.A. and U.K.

This was written and signed by a senior officer in his own handwriting. I'll let you draw your own conclusions, but now that we have a greater awareness of the need to be educated and vigilant about child sexual abuse, I don't think that response would have been written today.

– 9 –

Mick

My brother Mick was ordained a priest in 1968. He served in England and in the Cork diocese before opting to go to Peru to the Cork Mission. While out there, at the age of thirty-two, he got his first heart attack and was flown home to Dublin, where he underwent his first bypass. He had numerous bypasses after that but continued to serve his parishioners well. No matter where he went – Mayfield, Turner's Cross, Lissarda, Knockavilla – everybody had great time for him.

One night he was found collapsed on the floor of his house and was brought to hospital. He was diagnosed with Gillian Barrie Syndrome, a virus that attacks all the muscles in the body and causes paralysis; feeling eventually returns but it takes years to recover. The only movement he had was in his thumbs. He was in Lissarda at this stage and needed twenty-four hour attention, even in the hospital. His parishioners organised a rota of people to stay with him because if he needed to scratch his nose someone had to do it for him. He gradually recovered but it took nine months before he could say mass again. One of his big breaks came when he was able to go down to the pub in a wheelchair from the hospital and managed to lift a pint and drink it. His first day back in his parish, he was on the altar in his wheelchair when he said 'Here I am Lord', words which came to have a special significance. Each time I hear them it brings a tear to my eye.

Mick was a great man to get people to organise things for him. We would meet on a regular basis and he would announce from the altar that the Ryans were coming. Everyone knew what they had to do and by the time we arrived on the Tuesday, the table would be laid out and all the food ready for us, including delicious desserts.

Another time he saw his opportunity to gather a few pounds for the church in Mayfield. It was usual for bands to rehearse in the Country Club hotel on Mondays so he approached the owner and got permission to charge an entrance fee to see these bands in action. This lasted for a while and generated quite a sum for the church.

When Mick was in Peru, a friend of his, the musician Tomás O'Canainn, who was an amateur radio enthusiast, asked him to seek out a particular, similar enthusiast in Peru, up a mountain. Having found him it meant that Tomás and Mick could talk for ages in Irish over the ham radio and my father and the rest of the family would go down to Tomás' house and speak with Mick too. This was the 1970s, before mobile phones and emails. In those days we had a poor phone service and a letter took four weeks to get from Peru to Ireland. Tomás played with a group called Na Filí which was very popular at the time.

In 1973, he played at my sister Kathleen's wedding to Donal Connery, along with Matt Cranitch on fiddle and Mick Daly on guitar. They were brilliant.

On 23 September 1993, someone called to him at 2.40 p.m. but got no reply. My sister, Mary, had been talking to him just ten minutes beforehand and he was due to say mass that evening, but did not turn up. He was found dead in his front room sitting in his chair with his favourite Tazi music (French chanting) playing.

Whether I was on the beat or in the car, since my days on community policing I always tried to call to the nuns in Regina Coeli convent in Farranree. My colleagues and I were always made welcome there and spent many evenings in their peaceful and relaxing parlour. I would bring some of the lads up who wouldn't be the most religious but they too would be surprised at the welcome we would get. I always made it my business, working or not, to call to see them on Christmas Day.

As one of the nuns Sr Lelia was in Peru with my brother Mick, it was decided when he died that we would have a mass in the convent chapel. I asked my good friend Martin Sheehan to say the mass and I must say it was one of the most beautiful and intimate masses I ever attended. Martin had worked in Mitchelstown Creameries when I was stationed there as a security officer, so we were in constant contact with him and Mossy Joyce on a regular basis – great friendships which have lasted to this day.

Everyone held Mick in high esteem. Only lately I was in a shop when a man came up to me and asked me if I

Fr Martin Sheehan, John Riordan
and myself at Martin's first mass

was a brother of Fr Ryan. Mick had been the priest in this man's parish twenty years before, and he told me that Mick had a special prayer that he said after mass every day. Standing in the shop he recited the prayer for me, the ultimate tribute to my brother. In memory of him and all the people who knew him, this is the prayer:

May He support us all the day long
'Till the shade lengthen
And the evening comes,

And the busy world is hushed,
And the fever of life is over,
And our work is done.
Then in his mercy
May he give us a safe lodging
And a holy rest
And peace at last.
Amen.

My father had died in March 1978 and my mother in March 1980, so Mick joined them and was buried in Ballinaltig Graveyard, Watergrasshill.

– 10 –

My Best-Before Date

I have been fortunate in that I have only been in hospital three times in my life. The first time was with a suspected heart attack. I was getting violent pains in my chest and I went to the Bons Secour Hospital in Cork for various tests and a complete check-up. As I sat in the waiting room for results of the tests a nun came up to me and asked me to come with her. The nuns would have known my family history of heart problems as Mick always went to the Bons. I followed the nun and we arrived at the admissions office. I asked what was going on and she told me everything was okay and to sit into a wheelchair. The attendant took off, running down the corridor with me. We got the lift and arrived on some floor, and he took off running again with me until we arrived at the door of intensive care. I told him that I couldn't go in as I didn't have any clothes with me and, in any case, I had a meeting arranged with the lord mayor. I said I would come back after the meeting with some clothes, but he was not impressed.

In intensive care I was put onto a bed, surrounded with

monitors, and plugged into the machines. Nobody said a word to me about what was happening. A few minutes later, I was unplugged, wheeled into the isolation ward and left there. Shortly after a priest came in to ask after me. I told him my story, and my only consolation was that he didn't anoint me so at least I knew I wasn't on the way out. It transpired that my gall bladder was causing the trouble, so I underwent microsurgery to have it taken out.

When I woke up I was in a semi-private room, with another man, Paddy Daly from Farranree, with whom I had a lot in common, such as both loving going to Murphy's chipper in Gerald Griffin Street. We got on so well that I called to him and his wife Betty when I was on the beat and we still meet and have a good old natter.

The next time I succumbed to illness was when I got back from Nigeria, where I went for the under-20 World Cup. I noticed that I was very tired and would fall asleep easily. I was also drinking a lot of water. I found night duty the hardest and often fell asleep around 2 a.m. The girls on the unit, Caroline Nolan and Laura Dillane (both now sergeants, I trained them well!), would often have a bet to see if I would make it through the night without falling asleep. We often talked about it and came to the conclusion that it was not normal. I went to my doctor and blood tests revealed blood sugar levels of twenty-five when in fact they should have been between three and seven. I was rushed to hospital and taken to the diabetic ward in Cork University Hospital where I was put on medicine and a diet to regulate my sugar levels. It appears there could be up to 750,000 diabetics in this country, unaware of their condition, perhaps like me thinking they have just picked up some bug.

As circulation and lack of sensation in the limbs is poor, diabetics have to take care of their feet. I had a little trouble with mine and had to attend the podiatrist. You also have to be careful with your eyes and get them tested regularly. The first time I got this done, I didn't realise that the drops used would blur my vision and I came out, sat in my car and drove home. It was a stupid, crazy thing to do and I never did it again.

My last foray into hospital was when I was having a problem with my toes and was brought in for a minor operation on an ingrown toenail. When I was brought down to theatre, I was told it was going to be a local anaesthetic and to lie back. But I wanted to see that needle going in so that there would be no surprises and I could psyche myself up for the pain so I sat there and watched the full operation, much to the amusement of the surgeon and his staff. I was put in the recovery room for all of five minutes and then back to my room where I had to put my leg up for a couple of hours. In all I was in there for ten days, and had the most relaxing time. I came out of there totally refreshed.

One night while I was walking around the hospital, and on the way down to the kitchen to make some tea and toast, there was a flurry of excitement on the corridor as the nurses came rushing along with a man up on a trolley. They took him into a ward of six, pulled out the inside bed with an elderly man on it and put him against the wall facing the door.

I stood at the door of the kitchen opposite the ward and watched as the nurses worked furiously on the man they had just brought in. It looked serious. I threw a glance at the old man in the other bed and thought to myself that he was dead. A nurse looked at him, but returned to working on the other man. My attention then focused on the elderly man and I decided he was definitely dead. The nurses were so busy with the other man that it took them a couple of minutes to discover that in fact the elderly man was indeed dead. I spoke to one of the nurses the following night and she told me he was definitely alive when they moved him and that the same man was wishing himself to die for a month beforehand.

Lately, I was in the diabetic clinic in Cork University Hospital where the procedure is that you give a urine sample and then you are weighed. You would not need to go to medical school for five years to see that I was overweight. I don't have a problem with my weight, but everyone else apparently has. The nurse put me on the scales and said, 'Oh, you are a bit overweight.' I said I had no problem with it and that I have no problem with the diabetes. I told her I had a great life getting this far, and I had no idea when I was going to die as the day I was born, no-one put a best-before date stamp on my arse, so I had nothing to gauge how long I had. In any case, I said I did not want to end up like them, pointing to all the people in the waiting room, who were petrified and all looked like they were facing a firing squad. As far as I was concerned they were worrying themselves to death. She looked at the people, looked at me and smiled and said, 'Maybe you are right.' I then went and met the doctor, who was from Pakistan, and who wanted to give me a lecture, but I sidetracked him about Ireland and Pakistan who had played a hockey match that day. He told me that if I'm not careful I would be injecting myself shortly and that I was to do this, that and the other and then he said 'come back in a year'. I said, 'That's fairly urgent all right.'

– 11 –

WATERCOURSE ROAD

We had a great unit in Watercourse Road and had great craic on our shifts, especially on nights when there was no 'brass' around. We would often adjourn to Mayfield station and have a few great games of cards – poker or 110. We used go to a Chinese chip shop in Blackpool known to us as Bobby's; no-one was sure of the owner's name so he was christened Bobby. I was there one night when there was trouble amongst the customers. As I went into the shop they all wanted to have a go off me. They were taunting me with personal insults so I told them to wait and I would get a 'real' guard for them. Mick Hanley was about 6'6", and when he put on his motorcycle helmet he looked like a giant. I called him on the radio as I knew he was nearby, and he arrived quickly. I told the crowd that they would get no satisfaction hitting a small fellow like me but to hit Mick instead. You never saw a crowd disappear so fast. He was a mighty man to have with you in a difficult situation.

Around this time my old friend Terry O'Sullivan, who had served with me in Ballyconnell, arrived in Watercourse

Road and it was like the old days. Unfortunately he was set upon by a mob one night, received serious injuries and had to retire on medical grounds.

John James, otherwise known as Jessy, then arrived in the station party. On his first night off we went on the beat in Blackpool and nearly forgot to come back so engrossed were we in conversation about GAA, soccer, rugby and, of course, garda matters. One night on the Common's Road, we were out in the patrol car when we were rammed by a stolen car. These fellows don't give a damn. We were lucky in that we survived with just back injuries. At least it happened on the Common's Road, not like a few years previously when a patrol car was crashed into out in the countryside – far from where it was supposed to be patrolling! Perhaps the garda was visiting friends. A quick-thinking colleague got it towed back and put it up against a pole in the Common's Road, saving the guard a lot of explaining and writing.

One of the saddest things Jessy and I witnessed was on one Christmas morning at about 4 a.m. when we got a call to a family row. On arrival, the wife told us that she had a barring order against her husband but had met him that evening downtown. They had gone for a few drinks, got on well and she asked him back to the house. They got on so well that they went to bed, but at some stage the man decided he didn't want to sleep and started to beat her up. He then went downstairs and destroyed all of Santa's toys which they had put out together earlier. So here we were, on Christmas morning, trying to console six- and seven-year-olds whose toys had been destroyed. I subsequently came across these kids and unfortunately they now have the same attitude as their father.

I had a green Mercedes at that stage and one night, while parked outside the station, it was hit and written off by a Fiat Punto. The driver got into his car and drove away, never to be found again. Two girls passing by had taken the number of this offending car and given it to two gardaí at a checkpoint in the city. The gardaí listened, then told them to go away and mind their own business, so the girls did. By the time I tracked them down, about a week later, they had thrown away the offending car's number. The checkpoint gardaí obviously did not care about the car and had done nothing about it. I had to shell out myself for the car as I had just changed my insurance from comprehensive to third party. Two valuable lessons learned.

One thing that really got up my nose was spitting. I don't mean spitting discreetly, but when someone spits at you or across you. It's disgusting. One day an aggressive prisoner was in the back of the paddy wagon and as he was getting out he spat right into my face and said that he was HIV Positive. He later said that he wasn't, but we had to check with the hospital who were satisfied that he didn't have HIV. It was a worry for a while.

On another night I arrested this arrogant, obstructive guy for something or other. He refused to give me his name and just kept spitting across me. I told him to stop, but of course he didn't. I said, 'If you don't stop, I will make you lick the floor.' He continued so I got him onto the floor on bended knees and made him lick the floor dry. I don't think he will spit at a garda again.

When I first arrived in Watercourse Road there were only a few barring orders/protection orders (where one person gets a court order to stop their partner coming near them), but by the time I left we had a filing cabinet full of them. I always tried to be as fair as possible in dealing with situations that arose out of these orders but they could be tricky.

One night I got a call to go to a house where a disturbance was taking place. I had been there before and, on arrival, I found the woman out on the street, naked. Her husband had thrown her through the window. We got her some blankets to put around her and then went inside to arrest him. However, she went ballistic, saying we could not take him as she had no barring order. She was protesting so much and proclaiming her undying love for him that I really wondered what she was thinking. A month later we got a call to a different house, same lady, different man, who had also beaten her up. She still wouldn't make an official complaint, so we could do nothing.

In another case we got a call to a house about a barring order. We arrived to find the man in his working clothes sitting in the front room, watching television. I asked him what was wrong and he said it was his girlfriend who had rung us and that there was a baby upstairs. She had a barring order against him but he had been living with her for the past three months in breach of the order. There was no trace of the woman and he told me that she was fed up with him and was using the barring order to get him out of the house. After a few minutes the woman returned to the house and wanted the full rigors of the law to be administered. She hadn't bargained for what was to follow: I had no choice but to arrest the man and put him into the patrol car. As she was very drunk and was going back out for more drink, I asked her about the baby and she said her fourteen-year-old daughter would mind the child. I was not happy with that as the daughter was quite aggressive as well. I said I was taking the child and putting her into care. The mother said the baby wouldn't go to me, but I asked her to wait and see and went upstairs to the child. I smiled down at her, stretched out my arms and asked her to 'come to Jim'. She was adorable. She stood up in her cot and reached out to me. I took her to the car and handed her to the father and took both to the station. I put the child in temporary foster care and took the father to court, where I explained to the judge exactly what had happened and he let him go. I don't think that mother called the gardaí again about a barring order and I don't think she got another one again either. Judges have long memories.

I would always use what I called Section 100 of the Child Care Act to take children out of hostile environments. I don't think there is any such section but it always worked for me! We were forever getting calls to a particular house – a large family, mother and father fighting for thirty years, but still together. One Christmas Eve, I got a call to go to their house as they said it was a particularly bad fight this time. I decided that the only way to stop this fighting was to take the two youngest kids and put them into the car – Section 100 came in handy again. This had the effect of changing the situation from their fighting to pleading with me not to take them, but I felt I had no choice.

The kids came with me and a colleague in the car. We flashed the blue lights all the way so they were delighted with themselves. We took them at 3 a.m. on Christmas morning to one of the wonderful foster parents dotted around the city who, no matter what time you call, will have a smiling face for the kids. Once in care, the next morning, the health board was notified and they took it from there. Two days later I passed the parents and the two children and got a royal salute from them all as they walked peacefully into town. I never got called back to that house again.

At this stage I had moved to a new unit and was joined by, amongst others, Jerry White, Jim Worsley and the wonderful Renee Hurley, one of the first females to come to the city station. We got on very well with each other, and also with our sergeant, a lovely man called Mick Trihy. Jerry became a tutor garda, which meant he often had a student garda with him, willing to learn. It was great to have students with us as they were like retrievers or rottweillers. When we 'elder lemons' were unable to catch a gang we could unleash the student who always brought them back to us. One of the best 'retrievers' was Declan O'Keeffe, the Kerry football goalie who was super fit and streetwise.

At this stage I was living on Watercourse Road, and I used to have my car, an old Mercedes, parked on the street outside. One night around half three in the morning while I was working the night shift, I went over to the house. My car was parked across the street. While having a cup of tea, I got a weird feeling as I heard some guys coming up the street. I reckoned that when they saw the Merc, they would have a go at stealing it. As they got nearer I heard them crossing the road. I looked out the window and saw one of them at the door of the car and the other acting as lookout. I went down the stairs, opened the door gently and waited. I couldn't rush out onto the street as I didn't want to get knocked down by passing vehicles, but when I knew the road was safe I burst out the door and across the road and laid out my man who was at the door of my car. He pleaded that he was only going to the toilet. 'Not up against my car,' I said.

Now I had a problem, me on my own, two of them, and one set of handcuffs. I looked around. The other guy was amazed that they had been caught. I decided to do what I always wanted to do but never got the chance, and dragged the fellow who'd been by the car across the road, put one cuff on his hand, put it around the ESB pole and handcuffed his two hands together. I ran back to the station, called the patrol car and went back down the street to my friend attached to the pole. He was going nowhere but his buddy started to get cheeky so I told him he was in my town now and that if he wasn't careful he would end up attached to the pole like his friend. When Jerry and Jim arrived they saw the two lads and all they could do was laugh. I had done what I had to do, and this time avoided unnecessary damage to my car.

On the way to Mayfield, we discovered that the two lads were from South Hill in Limerick and that they had plenty of previous convictions. I told them that they were very unlucky on a few counts: first, being in Cork, then trying to take a car that happened to belong to a garda, who happened to be on a break from work. The ironic thing is that it would have been hard to steal anyway, as it was a diesel car and the heater plugs need to be heated before the car starts. As they claimed they were injured by me, they were taken to the South Infirmary Hospital to be checked out. After an hour or so they disappeared, never to be seen again. Some do-gooder who was looking out a window that night and saw me handcuffing this guy to the pole reported me for hurting the poor innocent. An investigation followed but went nowhere as the two guys made no complaint. Another case of more sympathy for the criminals than the gardaí.

– 12 –

The Blackpool Shooting

I always loved being on the beat as I loved the freedom to walk around and meet people. I was never afraid, even when I was on my own. We usually went out alone. It's not ideal, but I suppose there was never enough personnel on a shift for a partner on the street. It was also nice to call to friends and have a chat and a cuppa with them. One Thursday night, 4 August 1995, Sergeant Mick Trihy called me aside to tell me that the inspector had asked him to keep an eye on me when I was on the beat as he thought I was skiving off. I was grateful for the warning. I headed off, went out to Blackpool and checked a few places, and then decided to call to friends of mine, Eddie and Eileen O'Brien, who lived in Farrancleary, just behind the flats. This was a regular haunt of mine and many's a good laugh was had in this house. I was just settling down to a nice cup of tea when I heard the inspector looking for Mick Trihy on the radio. That was my queue to leave, so I excused myself. It turned out to be a dramatic night on the beat.

It was just coming up to midnight and I walked down

toward the flats (no longer there today) and onto a path running at the back. As I walked by one group of flats, I heard what I thought was a shot coming from one of the three groups of flats. I immediately notified Control of what I heard and told them to alert a car to head towards Blackpool in case I needed back up. We knew these flats well as there had been a murder there some time previously and we had had to watch them around the clock for about six months.

I went into the block of flats to investigate and was just standing in the courtyard when a shot rang out and whizzed passed my head. I dived to the ground, not knowing where the shot had come from. I managed to crawl to the wall of one of the flats, and I notified Control that I had been fired on but was o.k.

I still didn't know where the gunman was so I started crawling along the side of the flats, back to where I had been. Standing in a doorway was a man I knew and he pointed to me that the gunman was on the first floor balcony, on the block of flats behind me. I was talking on the radio all the time and receiving instructions. I told everyone to stay where they were and that I was going to make my way out to the roadway. Once out there, an idiot of a civilian came along and said he was going to go in to deal with the gunman. I tried to stop him but he got away. By now the inspector had arrived and I was just bringing him up to speed when another shot rang out. I thought my idiot had been shot.

A man appeared out of the dark from the flats, shouting that he had been shot. It later transpired that, even though there was blood flowing from his hand, he hadn't been shot but had cut his hand on a broken window. At this stage an ambulance arrived and took him away before he got into more trouble. The inspector said he would go and notify the super about what was going on. He never again questioned whether I was on the beat or not.

There was a stand-off for a while until we discovered that the gunman was holding everyone hostage in a pub up the road. The bleeding man had unintentionally caused a diversion while the gunman got away. My colleagues, Jerry White and Jim Worsley, arrived on the scene and we approached the pub on Thomas Davis Street. A local came out waving a white handkerchief and told us that the gunman was inside and wanted to talk to the gardaí. Jerry and I were just about to go in the door when he appeared and pointed the gun at us, then at his head and then into his mouth. He beckoned us to go back. At this stage the Special Branch personnel had arrived but they were hidden down the street behind us. The gunman kept repeating his actions with the gun to the head, to the mouth and then at us.

He walked backwards up the street, still holding us at bay with the gun pointing at Jerry, Jim and me. At this stage I felt I was facing death and could be shot dead at any moment. He looked very nervous, quite mad and agitated and as if he was capable of anything. I felt some kind of adrenaline rush which had my senses on full alert. He tried to stop a car but it kept going. As more and more people came out onto the street we became increasingly worried, as we didn't know what he was going to do next and he could easily shoot at any of them. As we approached the grotto at the bottom of Dublin Hill, he again tried to stop a car which this time he succeeded in doing and got into the passenger seat. Jim and Jerry ran alongside the car, one on either side, getting the driver out and struggling with the gunman to get hold of the gun, which they did. They handed the gun to me and arrested him. He turned out to be a well-known Cork criminal.

We put him into the patrol car to bring him to Mayfield station and found that in the middle of all the drama some smart ass had managed to get into the car and plaster the steering wheel, gear handle and anything they found with chip grease. Someone thought it was funny, but it was extremely difficult to drive the car at this traumatic time.

We finally got to the station and put the gunman into a cell. Soon after that the impact of the event started to have a physical effect on me. I hadn't felt a lot of fear at the time but later my head became enveloped in the most uncontrollable sweat, which lasted for a few days. In fact from time to time I still get the symptoms: the sweat just comes on all of a sudden and my head and hair end up completely wet.

I went back to the scene and was told that I was to stay there until morning to ensure nothing was touched. No one asked if I felt all right or checked whether I needed to go home, even for a cup of tea. In fact, no-one in authority has ever asked me if I was o.k. and had I coped with this stressful event. After all, we had been threatened by a gunman and one false move could have led to a loss of life, perhaps our own.

I went home that morning at 6 a.m., finishing my shift as if nothing had happened. I went to bed but could not sleep. I kept thinking of what could have happened.

Civilians were very kind to me and indeed still ask me how I am after that awful night I 'got shot'. When I had returned to the scene there was a photographer there clicking at everything he could see. I asked him not to take a photo of me but he still took the picture. Because of the way I was moving my arms to stop him, it looked like I was covering my heart. This picture appeared on the front page of the *Evening Echo* and people assumed that I was shot in the heart. Even last week a man asked me if I had recovered from the time I was shot. I had been shot *at*, not shot, but that two-letter word didn't make much difference when the photograph suggested I had been.

The criminal was charged the next evening and it appears he never realised it was a garda he shot at. When he saw my photo in the paper he sent word to me that he was sorry, as he said he liked me. Why he liked me, I'm not sure, but perhaps he saw me as a fair garda. How strange it is that I got no help from my authorities, yet an apology from the criminal! One sergeant told me that nothing much had happened and that I was making a big deal out of the situation. He would have appreciated the ordeal if he had ever had a gun pointed at him. Recovery from the trauma was not helped by insensitive remarks from superiors who should have known better.

I was very bothered for a good few days and what bothered me most was the fact that I was bothered by the whole situation! I was always a very easy-going fellow who rarely got worried about anything, so I was a little concerned until one day, a few days after the incident, when I met my sister Kathleen. We went for a long walk and talked it all through and I felt better after that. You don't always know exactly what is bothering you until you tell someone else about it. Delayed reaction is often harder to recognise as it comes without explanation. In my case, it came later that night in waves of fear and sweat and then days later when I wondered if I was losing my confidence and courage. Not ideal in a guard.

One day soon afterwards I was sent to the prison to escort prisoners down to the court. I never realised that my attacker was going to be one of the prisoners and I froze when I saw him. I think he got a shock too. In fairness to one of my colleagues, he copped what had happened and started talking to me non-stop about hurling, football and soccer – anything to take my mind off him. I refused to accompany the prisoners back to the prison afterwards.

The criminal was sentenced to eight years for firing at me and for possession of a firearm. I was never told when the trial was on, but a sergeant who was not at the scene during the incident but had arrived a few hours later when it was all over, gave evidence that it was one of the most dangerous nights that he himself had been involved in with the Garda Síochána.

A lot of people thought Jerry, Jim and I would be highly commended or maybe even get recommended for Scot Medals, but nothing happened until the same sergeant was going for promotion about two years later. We were asked, as per the usual regulations, to sign a recommendation for Scot Medals, me for keeping my cool and helping to direct traffic in a very volatile situation – nothing about the bullet that barely missed my head whizzing past. We signed but never got the medals. However, the sergeant got promoted. All I received from the whole situation was bad hearing, anxiety attacks and no sympathy.

– 13 –

BSE Watch

In 1996, six months after the Blackpool shooting, there was an outbreak of BSE and the border with Northern Ireland was sealed off. I was summoned to the sergeant's office and told I was going to Dromad in Co. Louth for a few months. We had a good 'discussion', which of course he won, and ended with him saying to me, 'Jim, all this is for your own good.' I replied: 'Every bollocks that ever stabbed me in the back told me it was for my own good.' All my family and friends were in Cork and I didn't want to go. I took it to the super but he would not budge even though Brendan was doing his Junior Certificate exams at the time which would usually have been a reason for flexibility.

I arrived in Dundalk and was told I was going to be stationed in Dromad, which is on the main Dublin to Belfast road, but with many crossings in the sub-district. I think it was the first time that every crossing between North and South was covered. I settled in o.k. but was not happy and bitched at every opportunity, thinking someone might send me back to Cork, but it wasn't to be. The duty was boring: on a checkpoint from 7 a.m. to 3 p.m., 3 p.m. to 11 p.m. and 11 p.m. to 7 a.m., on your own except if you were on the main road where two guards were on duty.

It was fairly eerie out in the middle of nowhere. One night, as I patrolled the road, I heard breathing quite close to me, quite heavy and persistent and frightening. In the dark it took me quite a time to realise that some cattle were curious about the Cork guard.

Another day while on another checkpoint I spotted a herd of cattle walking down the road from the North on their own. Obviously they had heard that the South was BSE-free and so were coming south for a holiday. I put a stop to that notion and herded them back north.

I got on well with the locals and some of them used to feed us; in fact one family looked after me very well and would bring me into their house for tea and cakes while their young son manned the checkpoint for me. One Saturday morning, I was on this checkpoint, on the road to Jonesboro, when a car approached. When the occupants saw me they stopped about 100 yards back. I put my hand up to signal them to stop but they revved up and came at me. At the last second I jumped out of the way. It transpired that they had robbed the post office in Ravensdale about two miles away.

I was in Dromad during a very turbulent time, both North and South. In Adare, Co. Limerick, our colleagues, Jerry McCabe and Ben O'Sullivan, were ambushed by an IRA gang and shot at indiscriminately, Jerry receiving fatal wounds and Ben miraculously surviving. This shocked the whole country and is still a contentious issue. Around the same time, Veronica Guerin was shot dead in her car near Newlands Cross in Dublin. These were two of the most high profile murders to occur in the state.

Up North there were riots in Portadown and on the Garavahy Road near Drumcree. They spread all over the North coming up to 12 July 1996. On the night of the twelfth there was no traffic, owing to the riots, and people were advised not to travel to the North. Dr Joe Henderson, MP, of the SDLP, approached the checkpoint and I advised him not to go up as I had heard there was a mob on our side of Newry, hijacking and burning cars. He said he would be okay, but I insisted he, of all people, should wait till daybreak and then go up. He eventually took my advice.

The Northerners were very nice to us on their way South, but it was a different story when they were heading home: they would abuse and hurl objects at you. I decided to address this problem by narrowing the road and stopping everyone of them so they couldn't throw anything at me. This worked for me so I did the same with lorries going North; narrowing the road with cones until they slowed down, though the only way to really slow them was to narrow it so much that they ended up driving in the drain. It was while on a checkpoint on a back road that I saw and used my first mobile phone. A man came up to me, talking on his big apparatus and later showed me how to use it, allowing me to telephone home. It seemed an amazing invention. I liked the idea of being able to call home while I was on duty and check up on the times of matches.

I was on the main road on some bitterly cold nights. We used to be on duty all night so I brought a chair into the middle of the road and settled into it with my legs up on a few concrete blocks. Suddenly a big lorry was beside me with the driver talking down to me, asking if it was okay for him to carry on up the road. He must still be smiling to himself about the guard asleep in the middle of the road in freezing weather.

It was important at that time to check all storage vehicles and if we found anything to contact the Department of Agriculture. One day, at 5 p.m., a lorry stopped and as usual I asked the driver to open the back door of his truck. He said he had beef burgers in there so I had to pull him over and contact the department. The vet had to come from Dundalk about eight miles away. At approx 7 p.m. a patrol car came up to the checkpoint followed by another car, which I thought was the vet. I went over to the car and greeted him, explaining about the lorry and the burgers. 'Great, well done,' he said, but he was not inclined to go over towards it. I asked him if he wanted to see the burgers or talk to the driver, but he declined. It turned out he was the assistant commissioner and got a great kick out of my error. The vet arrived later and okayed the lorry to continue down south.

I spent two months in Dromad but I wasn't happy there: not the place, just the circumstances. I missed seven international games and I had to drive up and down to Cork, often leaving at 3 p.m. and returning next day for 3 p.m. duty.

One Sunday one of the lads, who was a referee, asked me to umpire a match with him. It was an Armagh county senior hurling semi-final in Keady in Co. Armagh. We arrived at the venue and I took up my position at the goals; I didn't know who the other umpire was. The match was on only a few minutes when a ball went wide at the other side. With that the defending team started hitting hurleys off the goalpost, barely missing the other umpire. I didn't know what was going on but it transpired that the other man had been county secretary and had been involved in suspending some of their players. We got out of Keady alive, but it was a hair-raising experience.

It reminded me of an incident when I was a young fellow of fourteen and a friend, John O'Mahony, was a referee. We went to Riverstown one night to do a match. The match was B grade football between two local teams. The match was okay, nothing too much happening, until John had occasion to put one fellow off. His team took great exception and blamed John for losing the game. They went to physically attack him and he had to take refuge behind seating inside the field. It got pretty nasty but we eventually got him and ourselves into a pub next door. We heard the commotion outside and looked out to find a big crowd trying to overturn John's car. We had to call the guards to get us out and escort one of the lads to John's car. The club was suspended for ten years for this, but was back playing again within two years. A GAA solution to a GAA problem.

– 14 –

Dealing with Accidents

When I was a young fellow growing up in Watergrasshill, there was a butcher's stall down the street and up the back was the slaughterhouse, where they killed the cattle and sheep. At that time they were allowed to kill the animals with a humane killer: shooting a blank bullet into the brain of the animal. This knocked them out and they would then slit the throat and the blood would pour out. It was a good training ground for me as a garda when I had to go to the scene of the most gruesome and bloody accidents you could imagine.

When you arrive at the scene you have to be strong; there is no point in being in charge and feeling sick. I can still see the horror on the faces of two victims in a double fatal accident. One could obviously see the accident happening but could not do anything to prevent it. The other, a drunken driver, didn't know anything about his last moments.

Another fatal accident involved a pedestrian who was knocked down. He was in an awful state, bleeding badly. Another garda and I kept him alive for about forty minutes until the ambulance arrived but he died on the way to the hospital.

In this country everyone who dies has to be certified by a doctor. If someone dies suddenly as a result of an accident, suicide or murder, or has not visited a doctor for a number of months, a post-mortem has to take place.

I never had a problem going to post-mortems; I was always fascinated by the way the body works and never found it gruesome. I knew guards who never went into the room, in spite of the fact that a garda is always required to be present at all times once a relative identifies the body to the garda and in turn to the pathologist.

One victim was shot and I was flabbergasted with where the bullet ended up. It entered the body near the heart and it took the pathologist a while to find it at the base of the victim's back.

One thing I learned about death was that none of us knows what happens behind closed doors. Three sudden deaths come to mind to illustrate this. The first case was a woman who died in her house. Her son was able to tell me exactly what time his mother died, as he knew what time she cleaned each room in the house and when she would have been in the room where she died. The next was a man who died in his bed. He and his wife had not spoken for years and slept in different rooms. As far as the neighbours were concerned they were a very happy couple, so when the neighbours called to pay their respects, I had to use all my powers of persuasion to keep them away from the room where he died. The third one was when I was called to a house and was told that the woman had not been seen for a few days. I went into the house and up the stairs and looked in the window over the door. I saw the woman lying on the bed; it was obvious she was dead. It became apparent that the woman had become a recluse in her own home and lived in squalor in one room, using a paint tin for a toilet. She had cut herself off from all her family and died alone even though her family lived in the same house. It was a sad case and a secret which that family has kept to themselves. When you get a call to a house in the middle of the night or at a time of sudden death, you get to see a hidden Ireland.

As I used to live quite close to the station, when we were on night duty on a quiet night, we often ended up in my house for tea. One night we got two calls, one to an accident and the other to a 'domestic'. Garda Caroline Nolan and I got landed with the accident which we knew would involve a lot of tedious paperwork. Garda Con Lucy and Garda Eamon Hickey went to the domestic, but as they were leaving the house they were approached by a man in a distressed state. He told them he had had a row with his partner and wanted them to go to his house with him. As soon as they entered the house they realised they had more than just a domestic on their hands. The partner was dead in bed with stab wounds. The lads did their job expertly and arrested the culprit and Caroline and I spent the rest of the night protecting the scene. This has to be done at all scenes of incidents to make sure the scene is not contaminated until Forensics and the state pathologist arrive to examine the scene.

The protection of a scene could go on for a few days and nights, as happened with another murder. We went from my house in the middle of having a quiet cuppa and watching the film *The Field* on television. I went with Tony Harnett while Mary Skehan and Ray Kerins went to another call which came in at the same time. Again we were called to what should have been a simple domestic and walked into a murder scene. We spent many nights in that house and one night I switched on the television and discovered that the couple had been taping the same film that we were watching when we got the call out – very eerie.

Another night Caroline Nolan and I were called to a disturbance and when we arrived one of the fellows had a cleaver and was wearing a balaclava. This man and his family had terrorised all the people around him. All the male members of the family have seen service in prison since. I remembered one Saturday evening many years before when all his kids were small. I came across them trying to strip a car on the side of the street. They were aged six, seven and eight – what a start to life! When he saw us he dumped the cleaver, but I had seen him. With the help of colleagues, we restored order and reported what had happened. This man has spent many years in jail since then.

– 15 –

More Stories from Watercourse Road

I loved being on the beat on my own with the freedom to walk and talk to people. There is a butcher shop in Blackpool village called Kingston's, where I used to deliver cattle and sheep with my uncle when I was a small boy. We would have great fun as some of the cattle or sheep would break away and we would give chase down the main street, which was also the main Cork to Limerick road. Little did I know that I would end up walking the beat in the same area. One day, while passing Kingston's, I noticed their sign outside with the laughing pig standing on two feet and his other two trotters up in the air. Some bright spark had got a marker and in big letters written my name over the pig's head. I took it as a great compliment that someone had recognised that I was the chief pig.

I didn't always get away so lightly. At one stage when I was on the beat I would talk to Mary (not her real name). She thought this meant I fancied her, which I didn't. As time went on I noticed she was hanging around the station as I came and went to work. She started writing letters of undying love to me at the station and then to the sergeant about me. I ignored them but still they kept coming. She eventually discovered where I lived and started putting letters through the letterbox. At this stage it was getting to be serious stalking. She would wait near my house, so I had to watch out for her and take a different way home. She even started writing on the wall of my house, which was embarrassing. Eventually she got the message that I was not interested in her and left me alone.

Another family was friendly, but they got it into their heads that I had something against their son, who was serving time in prison. I had nothing to do with his convictions. One day the senior officer called me to his office and told me they were making complaints against me. He said I had not been nice to their son and that in future I was to treat him with respect. This senior officer didn't realise I knew that the father was very 'generous' to him with regards to 'little treats' from his workplace. The fact that I had been admonished by this senior officer meant that they had beaten me so then they really started on me. I would be walking along the road and they would drive near me sniggering. Or if they saw me driving they would go out of their way to walk across me, force me to stop and then spit on the ground in front of my car. If I was walking they would spit across me but they were always careful not to spit directly at or hit me. This went on for a long time until I eventually went to a different senior officer to report what they were doing to me. He didn't seem to take much notice of my story and in no time they were able to tell me that they knew I hadn't gained any satisfaction from my complaint and that I wouldn't be either. They continued at it so from then on I just kept well out of their way as it was clear I would not get any support from within the gardaí.

During the 1980s Siamsa Cois Laoi was a big success for the GAA. It was one of the first outdoor concerts to be held in the country and it generated a lot of cash for the Cork county GAA board. They put it to good use helping clubs to buy fields and build clubhouses and also bought development land for the county board.

One such ground was Flower Lodge, which was owned by the Ancient Order of Hibernia (AOH), and was considered to be one of the best football surfaces in Europe. The AOH put the grounds up for sale with a provision that whoever bought it would keep it as a recreational amenity. The GAA were approached and gave this undertaking, securing a prime piece of land for use as a second stadium for the Cork county board. It has since been developed to such a state that hurling matches can now be played there under lights, the first such facility in the country.

The Siamsas, which drew huge crowds, were great fun and great entertainment. They were always held during daytime on Sundays. I used to love being on duty all day long in Pairc Uí Chaoimh for those concerts as there was never any trouble at them and there was always the feel-good factor after them.

I remember one night after a concert being over in Anglesea Street station and you could hardly get in the front door with bodies. People who had got lost or had missed their bus were allowed to lie on the floor to have a sleep. We used do the same on the northside. At that stage McCurtain Street station was operating and most people who came to Cork knew where it was as it was on the way out of the city. We kept dozens of youngsters in the station until it was time for them to get an early morning bus or train.

With a capacity of nearly 50,000, Pairc Uí Chaoimh was used a lot for hurling and football matches. There were different kinds of duties to be performed for these matches. Non-public meant you were inside the ground and paid by the GAA and this was the one to get as you were able to see all the game. The other would be traffic duty: either directing or making sure people parked their cars properly. By 3 p.m. most people would be inside the grounds and there would be a mad scramble by the gardaí to get down to watch the match.

That is the great thing about Ireland: we are sports mad and even with 50,000 people all mixed together, there is never any trouble, with everyone enjoying the game. It is not unusual to see a garda in uniform getting all excited at a match, unlike English soccer where they have to face the crowd. We must be the envy of a lot of nations.

After the match it would not be unusual to see gardaí

doing 100 metre runs in ten seconds, back to their cars to get to their points before the crowds came out of the stadium. Then, later in the evening, you could meet people from other counties looking for their cars out in Blackpool. They wouldn't have a notion of where they had parked them, so I often had to 'interrogate' them to try to piece together information and get them to remember a landmark. If they said it was facing into the river the possibilities were numerous, but we always managed to locate the cars however many miles away from where they thought they had left them.

During the prison strike of the late 1980s, gardaí did duty in the prisons around the country. Watercourse Road subdistrict was part of Mayfield district and included in our sub-district was Cork Prison on Rathmore Road. Working there was a great opportunity to see how the prison system worked. At first the prisoners thought we would be a soft touch and would not be able to manage the running of the place. They were wrong; we took to it like ducks to water and in no time we had put our seal on the way we wanted to run the prison. The strike lasted for weeks and even though the hours were long – twelve-hour shifts, and we were used to eight hour ones – we really enjoyed it. It was completely different to what we were used to. The main problem was that the duty was confined to the walls of the prison which felt claustrophobic. I don't know if I would like to do it full time, but it was interesting while it lasted.

When the strike was over things went back to normal and I would only visit to serve summons, take statements and escort remand prisoners to the courts. Remand prisoners were ones whose cases had not come up yet and who could not get bail. A lot of these would be in custody for armed robberies, murders and violent crimes. One day, two of my colleagues and I took two of these guys to a provincial town for a remand hearing. I was told to be careful of one of them, as he was liable to do anything. On the way down I got talking to him and discovered he was quite personable. He was big into football, so he proceeded to do a Micheál Ó Muircheartaigh commentary on a match in which Cork had played a few weeks beforehand. His version was a bit skewed so I stopped him and got him to start again with a fairer assessment of the game.

We were brought in a side gate, so the press would not see us, but they knew there was a small gate where they all could get their photographs. As we came out of the van, the culprit spotted the photographers and played up for them. He kicked up a stink inside and abused the judge so we got the warrant very fast. He was an awful rogue and played to the gallery, cursing the judge, waving to the cameras, greeting his friends in the gallery, showing no respect for the court. We were rushed out the back door, traffic was halted to make way for us, we turned into the street and around the corner into a massive traffic jam and sat there for ten minutes. Nobody cared once we were gone from the courthouse and out of sight and we got back without incident.

All together there were three remand cases in the court that day for murder. A headline in the newspapers the following morning said: 'Three remanded on murder charge' and underneath was a photograph of the two lads and me in civvies. After that all escorting had to be done in uniform.

Another day I had to take a prisoner to another town. He and his wife were up for armed robbery of £20 and some sweets and chocolate from a petrol station. She was in custody as well. We arrived in the court where the wife got bail but he was remanded to the following day in a different court. I took him up to the local station where he asked me if his wife could visit. I agreed to it and when she arrived at the station I took her down to the cell area and supervised the visit. She was allowed to talk to him through a small opening in the cell door. He called me and asked me was there any chance that I could let her into the cell for, as he called it, 'a bit of nature'. I said 'not today' but that I would arrange it for the next day in the different station. This was a safe bet, as I knew I wouldn't be with him, but 'a bit of nature' was a new term to me.

One Christmas Eve, Des Renihan and I were on the beat when I saw a fellow in a chip shop. He was wanted for not returning to prison while on temporary release – I suppose you could say he was on the run. One thing I noticed is that fellows who are on the run never go too far away from home or else go to England for a few years and then come back, thinking no-one will know them. I was in Watercourse for over eighteen years, others were there for thirty, so a fellow would need to stay away for a long time.

When I noticed him I walked on and pretended not to care about him. Once down the street, I radioed for assistance. Luckily there were two patrol cars in the area, so I got one of them at one end of the street and the other at the other end. I approached the chipper and out he came and tried to get past me. He saw the patrol car at one side and we chased him into the other car. Before he realised I wasn't the idiot he thought I was, he was back in Cork Prison and had his Christmas dinner with the compliments of the state.

It felt a bit like when I was a young fellow and there was a sheep-dipping station in Watergrasshill. All the sheep in the area would be brought to this area and some would make a break for it. The knack was to catch them quickly and before they knew what was happening to get them dipped in this awful smelling liquid to keep them clear of maggots and other diseases. It didn't occur to me I was in training for the gardaí.

Part of our beat was McCurtain Street which was always very busy, as there was an all-night bowling alley on the street and a number of taxi bases. After the debs and graduation balls the youngsters all made their way to the McCurtain Street area. One such night Olivia Kelly and I were in the back-up car and patrolling the area, when we saw two girls and two boys in formal wear over by the river at Brian Boru Bridge on Patrick's Quay. I hated seeing kids fooling by the river so when the two guys went inside the barrier, towards the edge of the river, Olivia and I got out of the car and told them to come out. I didn't want to end up in the river at 3 a.m. just when I was due to finish work. One boy came out and said he was sorry but the second one said nothing and stayed standing at the edge looking into the water. I was worried he was going to jump in so I went inside the barrier. I asked him to come out and as I got near him he started using abusive language to me. I caught him by the coat and he hit me a belt into the face and spat at me. I started pulling him away from the edge but he punched me into the ribs. This six-foot two-inch nineteen-year-old was well built. I was rattled but determined he was not going to pull me into the river with him. It is amazing the strength you get with fear. As I pulled him more he continued to hit and spit at me. Meanwhile Olivia had called for assistance and was helping me try to get him to the other side of the barrier. Two taxi drivers saw us and stopped to give us a hand and as we got the boy to the barrier he head-butted me three or four times. At this stage other gardaí had arrived and between us we managed to restrain him.

I went to the Mercy Hospital later to get checked out and was fairly sore for a week or more . It transpired that the boy had gone to the debs ball with his ex-girlfriend as he wanted to get back with her. When she turned him down he threatened to throw himself into the river. The boy was to be charged with a number of offences including assaulting me, but nothing ever happened; he never went to court. He came from a very well-respected family who obviously had power and influence and got the whole thing shoved under the carpet. He did come to the station to say sorry but I knew he only did that because he was told he had to; it was not a sincere apology. Once more I was highly commended and recommended for an award for my 'heroism', but am still waiting.

Sometime later while on nights in the car with Ray Kerins and Mary Skehan, we got a call that there was a man on the phone to Control who was trying to kill himself. We got to his blocks of flats, rang all the doorbells, got into the building but could not find the right flat. Eventually we found it and I opened the door. We found the man inside with a sharp knife, trying to cut his wrist. I started talking to him but he was keeping us at bay with threats of what he would do if we came near him. We were joined by other members, which amounted to ten in the room – far too many. I got some of them to back off, so we were left with the three of us plus Richie Hogan, Tony Harriett and the man. I was the closest to him so I stood at the door of the bedsit, talking and trying to stop him from doing anything to himself. It transpired that he knew of me, which helped. I discovered he had children, so I worked on this angle, telling him if he did this it would be awful for the kids, especially as it was coming up to Christmas and it would ruin their Santa. I talked and talked like I never talked before, and promised him that neither I nor anyone else would hurt him.

I spent at least fifteen minutes talking to him and then, all of sudden, he handed me the knife and started crying.

I went over and gave him a hug and said I would look after him. He asked to be taken to Cork University Hospital, so we took him there and he signed himself in for treatment, and thanked me as I left. However good I felt about a fairly good outcome, I then had to call to his elderly parents and tell them where he was and his condition – not an easy task when you consider what a shock it must have been for them.

On St Patrick's night 1998, I was in the day room in Watercourse Road station. It had been a quiet enough day and I was getting ready to finish my shift at 10 p.m., having a chat with Con Lucy, now retired, and Peter Murphy. There was a bit of banter going on between us. The day room in Watercourse Road is a fine spacious room and I was sitting behind the desk in a swivel chair. The chairs in the station were provided by the Office of Public Works (OPW), who were responsible for furniture and buildings belonging to the state. If you were a manufacturer or builder and were in favour with the OPW you did well. It was a well known fact that when a builder put in a tender for a job, the idea was to quote as low as possible, get the job and add on as you go along. The chairs in our station were fairly standard, not the best of quality nor comfortable. As I sat in my swivel chair the whole thing collapsed and I fell backwards, getting stuck between the remainder of the chair and the wall. It looked funny, but I felt my neck and back getting sore. So now I had a bad back again, to add to my bad neck from the car being rammed and bad hearing as a result of the shooting incident. I had to received physiotherapy for many months after that, and still do from time to time.

The OPW and the manufacturers blamed each other for the chair but wouldn't replace the lot of them. Tests were carried out on them but all the others remained in place until another broke in the same way, this time while a senior officer was sitting on it. Then all chairs were removed from the station and much better quality chairs arrived within days.

My niece, Deirdre, who works with Irish Aid in Nigeria, got married in April 2001 in Nice in France. Her bridesmaid was her sister, Michelle, my godchild, who as a child had a reputation for biting dogs. The family headed over via Ryanair to Nimes. We had bought a Waterford Crystal chandelier for her and Basam, her new husband, and I had the job of getting it over to France as all the presents were to be shipped from there to Nigeria. I explained my predicament to the air-hostess, as I didn't want to put it through with the luggage. She took it and secured it in a seat with safety belts around it to keep it secure, and it arrived in one piece. Good service from Ryanair!

The wedding was an unusual one, held in a villa in an estate just outside Nice. When you arrived at the entrance to the estate, you had to identify yourself, and then you drove up the mountain where you were again greeted by security at the entrance to the villa. Outside the house were two Ferraris. We went in the back gate to the garden where there was a full-size swimming pool. A three-hour champagne reception followed, with real champagne for everyone, I'm assured. The wedding ceremony, attended by immediate family, had taken place the night before and this was a buffet style service. I went up to the long table and filled my plate, tucked in and finished it while a musical trio of guitar, fiddle and accordion played for each table. Then it was announced that the main courses were ready. I thought I had eaten the main courses – all ten of them, so I had to start again! During that course, we were entertained by a Lebanese belly dancer and I still cannot figure out how she was able to turn her body in so many different ways. A disco followed the speeches and toasts and it all finished at midnight, just as the Irish were in full swing.

While in Nice we visited Monaco, where I drove the Grand Prix circuit, visited the casinos in Monte Carlo and also went to Cannes where the rich and famous hang out in their top-of-the-range yachts. It was nice to live the life of the other half, even if it was only for a day.

On 22 April 2001, on my way to Nimes for the return flight I received the most shocking of news: two of my colleagues had been killed in a traffic accident on the North Ring Road in Cork City, while responding to a call for assistance from other members. George Rice, a native of Kilgarvan in Kerry, a gent of the highest calibre, was one of the most obliging men you could find, a wonderful colleague and a great family man. Seamus McIntyre, a native of Kenmare in Kerry, was a great hurler and footballer and a really nice guy from a garda background. He had really settled in well at Watercourse Road after his arrival from Galway.

I arrived at Stansted at 10 a.m. on the Monday, and anxiously waited for my flight home. I was too late for the removals but I was honoured when I was asked to say a decade of the rosary from the altar at George's reposing night in Matehy church. The crowds that attended the funerals were a testament to the popularity of both George and Seamus. As usual, a few gardaí tried to take advantage of a very sad occasion to further their own careers by trying to be seen as the chief organisers, but they were put in their place and dignified ceremonies continued.

George had often spoken to me about the possibility of taking his son Kieran to see Manchester United. I'm glad to say that, with the generosity of the gardaí and the help of a neighbour of George's, we got him to Old Trafford to see his favourite team play.

My unit was on nights the week following the funerals and I decided it would be nice if we went to the scene and said a few prayers, so we did. It was decided to put up a memorial to George and Seamus and that it should be put in the station as if it was erected at the spot of the accident it could be damaged or defaced. On their anniversary it was officially unveiled in a lovely ceremony in the station; this also revived the tradition of remembering our dead colleagues.

It was an unbelievable coincidence that twelve months to the day, and again on night duty, Brian Shanahan, who had replaced one of the lads on their unit, was at a scene of a minor traffic accident a couple of hundred yards from where George and Seamus died, when he was struck by a car which failed to stop. Brian was hit full on and thrown up in the air. With an amazing piece of luck, he landed on the grass margin. He received horrific injuries and was out of work for a long time but thankfully he survived.

In the gardaí when on the 'three relief' (our shifts) we worked a twenty-eight day roster. We would start our week of nights on a Monday night and there was always a full moon, which meant all sorts of strange and wonderful things would happen. I never believed in the full moon thing but at this stage of my life I think there might have been something in it. We would be busy most nights but extra busy on nights of the full moon; people always seemed to lose the plot.

One Monday night we got a call to a house on the northside of Cork city. This was a rented house occupied by a number of girls. When we arrived a few hysterical women met us. They worked in a city centre hotel, were off this particular day and had gone downtown to the pictures. They met a girl who they barely knew from work and asked her along. They all went to see *The Exorcist*. After the film they came home and brought the girl with them. All was o.k. for a while until she started seeing demons and tried to get rid of them by using a big knife. As the evening went on she got worse and locked herself and one of the girls into a bedroom and tried to perform an exorcism. With the help of an ambulance crew we eventually got her out and she was taken to hospital where I presume she received treatment.

During my thirty years of working as a garda I was involved in a huge number of incidents, from sudden deaths to murders, suicides, cot deaths, traffic accidents, shootings, sieges, larceny, assaults and just about everything imaginable. In the last two months of my service two incidents in particular disturbed me.

I have always been a critic of how the elderly were treated in commercial nursing homes, which I saw as money-making rackets providing very little service to those in their care. One night Garda Mary Skehan and I were called to one such place. On arrival, we met a very scared nurse and a more scared nurse's aid, who told us that one of the male patients was inside in an elderly female's room and would not leave. When I went into the room this gent was sitting at the side of the bed with his hands in under the sheets of the woman's bed. I asked him to stop and to leave the room and go back to his own room, which he did eventually.

I was concerned about the woman and called a doctor to have her examined. While I waited, I noticed a number of patients awake in their rooms. I spoke to one confined to bed who told me he had seen no one since 10 o'clock the morning before. The doctor arrived and examined the lady. She was fine, but it transpired that the man had a long list of similar offences in different homes around the country. Nobody had cared enough to check him out.

When the owner arrived she couldn't see what all the fuss was about and I had a job getting her to understand a few home truths about her responsibilities to care for the elderly.

The second incident happened a few weeks later, on a Saturday night. We had just come back to the station and were doing some work upstairs when we heard this loud bang downstairs. We rushed down and found a plate glass window broken in the station. We went outside and found a man standing outside the window. It was obvious he had thrown a rock at the window, so we brought him inside and sat him down. We talked to him for a while and it became clear he wasn't well. John (not his real name) told me he was a patient of a hospital in the city and that he wanted to go back in. I learned that John had not been well for years, and had been in and out of mental institutions all his life.

I was told there had been a bed for John in this hospital during the week but at the time he could not be found, and when he did turn up, the bed was gone. I telephoned the hospital and told them who I was, and who I had, but they told me they were full up and that another hospital was also full. We called a doctor who examined John and decided he needed treatment. On the way to the hospital John was quite happy and settled, knowing he was going to be looked after. We were directed to a waiting room where we sat until the night doctor arrived and took charge of him. We left John in good form at the hospital just after 6 a.m.

Next morning, I got a call from a garda supervisor who asked me what I had done with John. I told him we had left him in the hospital. The hospital had denied John was ever there. It transpired that after we left, the doctor examined John and he was then let out the door of the so-called secure unit (SU) of the hospital. He got a bus to a country town and was found dead in the river at 12.30 p.m. The hospital kept denying that John was ever admitted there. There was even a doubt I had taken him there. An enquiry was launched but I was never asked to attend so I don't know who got the blame. Maybe I did as I was retired a month later, so I could have been a handy scapegoat.

I was then given the task of meeting John's family and explaining to them what had happened. I had met them briefly the night before when John had broken the window as I had called to their home to enquire about him. It was sad and very frustrating and I felt powerless and angry at the hospital system. As we hear in the media these days, cutbacks and lack of an efficient and caring system played their part in John's death.

There are several of these SUs (houses where young offenders are kept, but are free to come and go as they please) in the Cork area. The young ones routinely went missing and we would receive a call from the SU to tell us. There is one such secure residential home in Dublin and some of our clients would be sent there. One Saturday morning two of us were dispatched there with a young thug who was normally very cheeky. He was very quiet on the way up and, just as we arrived in Dublin, he told us he would be back in Cork before us. The attendants have a legal obligation to make it clear to prisoners in this institution that they are free to leave at any time. This prisoner knew that.

We left the SU and headed towards Cork and had got as far as the Curragh when we got a call that our young thug had gone missing again. As soon as we were gone and he was fed and watered, he had headed off. The centre reported to their local station, who in turn contacted Watercourse Road. It was the fourth time he had done this and I'm sure he did so many times after. He was right. I saw him in Cork the next day.

The cost of this pointless exercise for a taxi from Cork to Dublin, two gardaí, probably on overtime, and other gardaí's time once he is caught again, made a mockery of the justice system. If you park your car in the wrong way you can expect at least a ticket, or to be clamped, which will cost you €80, and if somebody decides they need extra money you get towed away which will cost you €160 to get your car back. Meanwhile you have a system which gives criminals all the benefits.

– 16 –

Retirement

It was always my intention to retire when I had my thirty years of service completed in the gardaí. Martin Shanahan was my super at the time and I told him I was going and, what's more, I had picked a date: April Fool's Day 2004. Garda James M. Ryan 19496D became simply Jim Ryan and as I wrote in my diary on that date: *Retiring – free at last!*

It seems like a bit of madness expecting anyone to be interested in my life, but perhaps it's not everyone who has been a garda and not everyone who is fanatical about sport. I have been lucky enough to have enjoyed both and now that I am retired from the gardaí, I have the time to indulge my passion even more. I have been to as many football matches, at home and abroad, as I could fit in with my work as a garda, often reporting for 96FM from what for me have been exciting places and very enjoyable matches. The next section gives some insight into those travels.

Signing my retirement papers with (left to right) John Teehan, Claudine O'Sullivan, Olivia Kelly, myself, Brendan O'Leary and Eamon Hickey

– 17 –

A Sporting Life

I really had no choice but to be interested in sport. Watergrasshill GAA club has been my life from the age of four. All I ever wanted to do was be involved with the Hill and, even though I haven't lived there for thirty years, I never thought of going to any other club. There were times when I was tempted, owing to some of the narrow-mindedness of some members, but then I would talk to people in other clubs and they would tell me they were having the same problems. It's an Irish thing not to want progress.

Our sister club for football is known as Glenville and we were also successful with them, possibly more so than in the hurling, but hurling was my first love. It's only when you experience hurling that you can see what a great game it is. By a mile it's the best field game in the world.

I was ten years old when I first started playing hurling on the under-14 team, the first age group. By the time I was fourteen I was on the panel of the adult team, and played in my first adult final when I was fifteen. I was the goalie at fifteen; the corner forward was Frank Halbert, the former intercounty referee, who was in his late forties. We lost the game.

I was also involved in the administration of the club at this stage and was deeply involved in organising what we used to call carnivals. They were all the rage in the 1960s and 1970s: you had a marquee for dancing and Pongo (similar to Bingo), and a prize stall where you bought tickets and a wheel was spun to win the prize. There always had to be a hurling tournament too, where local teams took part and fought ferociously.

In 1974, the only year I didn't play with the Hill, they won the county junior hurling championship. Perhaps there is a moral in there somewhere. The same year the club bought its own field on the side of the main road. We were one of the first clubs to have its own land. We played at intermediate level for five years and were quite successful, but at the 1980 AGM we were relegated to junior level, where we stayed until 2004.

I was always interested in administration and was involved in different fundraising schemes down the years. I served as PRO on a number of occasions and as treasurer. In 1996, it was a special thrill for me to be elected chairman and I enjoyed three years in this position. In that time we won a few trophies on the field of play, and for two years we had people participating in the All-Ireland Scór competitions; Scór is the cultural side of the GAA and includes Irish dancing, recitation, singing, sketches and quizzes.

There was a lot of friction over my attempt to encourage the club to buy extra land for pitches. I was offered twenty-six acres, about half a mile from our pitch, for just under £100,000 – which would be worth about €5 million today. Some members couldn't look ahead to the future needs of the club and we are still involved in the same parish politics. Once in Athlone and the other time in Monaghan while attending the All-Ireland semi-finals I had to leave early next morning as the local soccer team was playing in a cup final in Turner's Cross. Contrary to the opinions of older members who disapproved of 'foreign' games and would like to have continued their ban of attending such games, I felt as chairman of the hurling club I should be there as most of these players played hurling with us.

Even when an idea is good, club members object because they put their own vested interests ahead of the club, hiding behind petty details and funding difficulties. With the expansion of the village, the need is even greater. The same problems still exist. This is just the kind of thing that frustrates me about the GAA.

– 18 –

All in the Name of Soccer

I have had my disappointments with the Irish soccer team – you need to be made of stern stuff to be a soccer supporter. One of my worst moments following the team was the away game in Brussels on 25 March 1981, a World Cup qualifier for the 1982 World Cup in Spain. We got a bus to Rosslare, a boat across the Irish Sea and then down to Dover for the ferry to Holland. On the way we got talking to two Limerick men, Tony O'Sullivan and Gerry O'Dwyer; this was to be the start of a great friendship between us that has stood the test of time.

The match was going well until seven minutes from time when Belgium got a dodgy free at the edge of the Irish box. The free kick ended up in the back of the net. It was a cruel way to lose and the only time I cried after a match. Later that year, I went to Rotterdam for the 2–2 game in the same competition accompanied by friends, Mick and Rose O'Connor, and a great man from Mallow, Dave Berry, who had a great passion for Southern Comfort whiskey liqueur. Each night he had to have two drops before going to bed, no matter what he had drunk all day. He lived to be a great age. Twice we went behind in scores and twice we drew level. This was the game that I got tickets through the Dutch FA and we were in the middle of the home supporters. When we got the second equaliser, I jumped with excitement and some local supporters took exception to this and landed a crate of beer down on us. We didn't care, we had got the draw.

Our final game in this series was when we met France in Dublin. We won 3–2 but it wasn't enough to qualify for the World Cup in Spain the following year.

In the next campaign we drew Holland again and headed off by bus for the long journey to Amsterdam. On this occasion, there was a ferry strike in England and we only barely got on a ferry to France instead of the boat to Holland. The hotel we were staying in Amsterdam was a kip: the first scene to greet us was a cat sitting on the breakfast table, and there were six-inch gaps in the doors so anything could roam from room to room. If that wasn't bad enough, Ireland lost 2–1, a bad start.

We also drew Iceland, Spain and Malta in this group. The match in Spain was held in Zarragoza in northern Spain. Zarragoza is a city with a huge number of churches and we visited most of them. The match itself was good, though we lost 2–0. The most memorable moment was when one of the Irish players, Ashley Grimes, was taken off and headed to the dressing room in disgust, but found he could not go in as the gate was locked. In view of us all he had to sit on the grass near the gate until the match ended.

After the game we went to the only nightclub in the city, and bluffed our way in by claiming we were Don Givens and Liam Brady. The club was later burned down and several people lost their lives.

≈ Germany for Euro '88

We arrived in Cologne in Germany at 2 a.m. on a Sunday morning for our first Euro '88 match. Our hotel was fairly central and we went off to bed as soon as we arrived as we had to be up again at 5 a.m. to head to Stuttgart for the big match, Ireland v England. On arrival at the stadium, it was like being at a match at home: so many familiar faces, full of expectations of taking on the old enemy. The match started well, and after six minutes Ray Houghton scored a great goal to take the lead and put us through the most torturous eighty-four minutes of our lives to secure a famous victory.

On the Wednesday we all headed onto the bus again for the long journey to Hanover for the game against Russia. I was designated map-reader and got us there in plenty of time. The match was a great game and I was privileged to see probably Ireland's greatest ever goal scored by Ronnie Whelan on the volley. The game ended 1–1. We now had three points out of four and were set-up nicely.

There was great craic in the hotel that night. The building was set out in three sections: in the middle was the accommodation, to the left was a brothel and to the right a transvestite club. It was the first time we had come across transvestites and we had great fun with them. They did not know what to make of us. One of them, who I had complemented on his singing, latched onto me and was very interested in me until I joked I was in a relationship with one of the lads from Kerry. He dropped me like a lead balloon. The brothel activities were very dull in comparison to what went on in that club.

We went on a cruise on the Rhine on the Friday night, and next day headed off to Gelzenkirchen for the last match in the group. We were full of confidence as all we needed to reach the final was a draw against the Dutch. Everything was going fine until the last ten minutes when Holland got a stupid goal which ended our dream. After the match, the Dutch and neutral supporters started to leave but, numbed at first, all the Irish stayed, and when a singsong started, the Dutch supporters returned to the stadium and joined in. We must have been there for at least an hour and both the team and supporters made their mark on world soccer.

≈ Italia 90 World Cup Qualifiers

Our next match was in Windsor Park, Belfast, against Northern Ireland; the first in the campaign to reach the World Cup finals in Italy in 1990. I made contact with an RUC member who secured tickets for us. Michael 'Fox' O'Connor from Tralee was with me. I had met him on the bus to one of our away trips and he is a mad man who doesn't need drink to have fun. John James, known as

Jessy, was with us too. He had recently arrived in Watercourse Road and I had struck up a great relationship straight away with him through our mutual interest in sport.

We took off in great spirits from Cork, but on the way north my car broke down and the two lads had to push. After a much longer journey than anticipated we eventually arrived in Dromore RUC station. Fox told the UDR personnel that he was from *real* republican territory, Kerry, and that we were from the rebel county. This information went down well and we got an RUC escort across Belfast in my Cork-registered car to Antrim Road. My contact had arranged for us to stay in the RUC station which had been bombed a few months previously. We were warned that if we went out, not to get a taxi back to the base, but to a garage across the road, as we could have been mistaken as RUC men.

We arrived at Windsor Park for the match and discovered that two of us were in the Linfield stand – a small wooden stand behind one of the goals – surrounded by very hostile fans who kept shouting 'ye Fenian bastards'! We thought the taunts were directed at us but discovered later that they were for the three Catholics on their own team. Jessy and I didn't speak to each other during the game to avoid drawing attention to ourselves and were very glad when the game ended in a nil-all draw. It was a very unfriendly place to be. When the match was over we walked out and got no hassle. We got back to base eventually and headed south, intact.

≈ 1986 World Cup

Many of the international trips we made were one-day jaunts which really took three days. Normally the flight would leave Dublin at 6 a.m., which meant we had to go to Dublin the night before, spend the next day at the match, then arrive back to Dublin in the early hours and either stay in Dublin or head for Cork, getting back at daybreak.

For the 1986 World Cup campaign we made a few of these trips as we drew the USSR, Norway, Denmark and Switzerland. Our journey to Switzerland was a memorable bus trip. We left Cork for Limerick, onto Dublin and down to Rosslare to get the ferry. We hadn't the brains to drive to Rosslare to meet the bus instead of doing a tour of Ireland.

We arrived in Paris on the Sunday and headed for Berne the next day where Tony Cascarino made his debut for Ireland. There was a bit of trouble at the match as some of the National Front got into the ground disguised as Irish supporters and had a go off the Swiss fans. Luckily the Swiss police realised early on what was happening and sorted it out.

The match against Denmark was the final one for Eoin Hand as manager of the Irish team. Public opinion forced him out after Ireland was defeated 4–0 in Dublin. The search then started for a new manager and, even though he was last choice with the FAI, somehow Jack Charlton got the job and so started a real rollercoaster of an era. Even though we had had great managers like Liam Touhy, John Giles and Eoin Hand, Jack had the luck that deserted the others up to that point.

Jack's first match was against Wales in Lansdowne Road, Dublin on 26 March 1986, a friendly, which ended in a 1–0 defeat. After this game we played Uruguay in a 1–1 draw, then it was on to Iceland for a three-team tournament with Iceland and Czechoslovakia, which Ireland won. David O'Leary was unable to attend; he had a family holiday booked before he was called up to the squad. Jack laid down the law and insisted on him going to the games but O'Leary refused and Jack disciplined him. Other players did worse deeds but Jack chose to ignore them. Jack then took it out on him by not playing him for a number of years.

≈ The Euro 88 Campaign

As I was involved with the Cork county GAA board in organising a horse-racing festival at Limerick Junction racecourse, I missed the first away game in the European competition against Belgium in Brussels, a 2–2 draw. The idea for the races came from the fact that Listowel Races were on after the All-Ireland football final, but there was nothing on after the All-Ireland hurling final. Liam Cusack and I put a plan together to hold a GAA-organised race meeting and submitted it to the Cork county board.

Cork defeated Galway in the hurling final and got our racing festival off to a great start. It worked so well in 1986 that we had a two-day meeting with plans to extend it the next year. However, without informing us, someone pulled the plug and it faded away.

Ireland got off to a good start in the European campaign: after that 2–2 draw against Belgium, Scotland came to Dublin and we drew nil-all. The match in Hampden Park in Glasgow was won with a Mark Laurence goal, so we were going well. Tony and I headed for Sofia again, where we were beaten 2–1 and got the mother and father of a wetting while watching the game. Later that month we drew nil-all with Belgium in Dublin. In May that year in Dublin, we played Brazil and Liam Brady scored a wonderful goal for a 1–0 win over the Brazilians. Five days later, we beat Luxembourg in Luxembourg, and in Dublin in September we beat them again, 2–1. In our last game in the series we beat Bulgaria 2–0 at home. Liam Brady was sent off and it cost him dearly as he got a very severe suspension of four matches; this forced him to miss the first finals that Ireland were to take part in.

Now all we had to do was wait and hope against hope that Scotland, who were out of the championship, would do us a favour and beat Bulgaria in Sofia – a feat that no country had succeeded in doing up to then. But miracles do happen and thank god for Saint Gary McCoy who scored a goal for Scotland which put Bulgaria out of the competition and put us in.

Our next game was the away game against Spain in Seville. There was a great atmosphere in the ground and our lads really took the game to the Spaniards, so much so that the Spanish supporters were beginning to turn on their own team. Unfortunately the Spanish scored an opportunistic goal and the supporters' attitudes changed completely. They then got another goal for a 2–0 win. After the game we were taken straight back to the airport. We boarded the plane and were taxing down the runway when the pilot, a very funny man, announced that a few bodies were late and he was going to wait on the runway for them. The three lads were brought out to the runway by car, the plane doors opened and the lads jumped in, to the sound of a big round of applause. We arrived glumly back in Dublin and faced the long journey to Cork, arriving in time for work at 6 a.m.

≈ Italia '90 – the campaign continues

The road to Italia '90 had started with that nil-all draw in Belfast in September 1988, and continued in Hungary in March 1989. The guys and I flew over for the match to Budapest, a lovely city divided by the Danube into Buda and Pest (the old city). We drew nil-all. Just as we were coming out of the match we were mugged and our hats and scarves taken. This ruined an otherwise pleasant trip as I had had both my hat and scarf for a very long time.

These matches were followed by four home wins against Spain, Malta, Hungary and Northern Ireland, before the final game of the group against Malta, which I missed. We won 2–0. After so many near misses we had finally qualified for our first World Cup finals.

The country was electric as June 1990 approached. Once more we were drawn in our first match against England in Sardinia, followed by Egypt and Holland in Sicily.

I booked our trip with a travel agent in Dublin who promised us the trip of a lifetime surrounded by sand, sea and good football. On arrival in Palermo Airport we were transported in the middle of the night to our apartments, which we were not near the sea as we expected, but about a mile up a mountain from the village of Cefalú, about twenty miles from Palermo.

When we got to the apartment, the two Limerick guys, Tony and Gerry, took over the bedroom and left the poor, naïve Cork fellows, Jerry and I, to make up our own beds in the sitting room on the floor. They regretted it later as the heat was stifling and they had no window in their room; we were able to open the doors to allow the air to circulate.

For the first match we were due to go by catamaran from Palermo to Cagliari in Sardinia. The trip to Sardinia took eight hours and not the four we had been told and we arrived at 7 p.m. really tired and hungry. At this stage we had to make our way straight to the grounds for the 9 p.m. match. I stopped a bus and the driver took us to the grounds, going out of his way to get us there. We had bought good tickets at £56 each which were in the top deck of the stand with a great view. Unfortunately the skies opened and we were soaked to the skin. We later discovered that those who had bought the cheap tickets were in the stand underneath us and felt no rain. The match was a good game and ended with a 1–1 draw.

Our return trip was even worse, with a storm breaking the radar and causing the ferry to nearly capsize. Luckily enough, there were two boats, so the other boat towed us back to Cagliari. The following morning we set off again in much calmer seas to Palermo but failed to get into the

Holland v Egypt game. Our apartment was so far from the sea that each day we had to take with us whatever we needed for the full day and night. One day we went to the nearest shop to buy butter but it was so hot that by the time we got back to the apartment it had melted completely.

The village of Cefalú was lovely and the sea there was very calm, so one day four of us (Tony, Ger O'Gorman, John Magnier and I) hired out a paddle boat. It was pure heaven, with blue skies, gentle breeze and constant sun. At one stage, two of us got into the sea and the other two in the boat pulled us along. When it was time to change positions though we couldn't get back up onto the paddleboat. I went down under the sea and somehow came up again and it was only then we discovered how far out from shore we were. The lads told me to get up on the paddleboat which at this stage was upside down. As I clamoured up, my leg went straight down through it. We waved frantically for help but all we got back were cheerful waves. Eventually someone realised we were in trouble and the owner of the paddleboat came out to rescue us. The next day we went out again, but were much more careful.

The next match was in Palermo against Egypt. This was as bad a game as you are likely to see, ending nil-all. That was the game for which Eamon Dunphy had a go at Jack Charlton, with the result that after that Charlton refused to answer questions from Dunphy ever again.

The day after the game we hired a car and headed up to Mount Etna, the volcano, which was an amazing sight.

At the bottom of the mountain it was 80°F and at the top of the mountain it was -20°F, but you were still not cold as the burning lava gave off heat. It was amazing to see all the lava burning on top of the ice, not melting. On the way back we crossed some of the highest bridges I have ever seen; our little car was shaking from side to side.

Our final match in the group was against our old friends the Dutch. They took the lead and Niall Quinn equalised. After that you could see the players talking to one another, knowing that both teams would get into the next phase. England had beaten Egypt, and so the three teams from our group would go through.

The word that week was that we would be playing Romania in Genoa. Our travel agent said it would cost us £1,000 to get there – an enormous amount. Tony and Gerry said they would go, but Jerry and I decided to come home and try to get out again on a separate trip as we felt it would be cheaper. We failed to get a return ticket as the travel agents here also wanted to charge a fortune, so I went back to work. I was SO on the Monday evening when the match came on television and missed loads of it as a woman came into the station on some trivial matter. She kept apologising for delaying me, and I told her that I had been to Italy for the match hoping this would hurry her up, but to no avail. Eventually she left and I got to see the extra time and the famous penalty shootout.

The following morning I tried everything to get out to Rome for the match against Italy in the quarter final but again, the travel agents tried to take advantage of the urgency.

I wasn't as cute then as I got later on, so I ended up in the Silver Springs Hotel looking at the match on a big screen and we lost 1–0. I couldn't understand the jubilation. I was deflated as I felt we should have won the match, but here were all these people jumping up and down, the better for drink and happy the score wasn't worse. I swore I would never go to such a place again to watch a match.

So Italia '90 ended.

– 19 –

The Road to USA 1994

The 1992 Euro campaign did not go very well, even though it had started well with a 5–0 win in Dublin against Turkey, followed by a 1–1 draw against England. We failed to qualify and I was lucky enough to have missed the last match against the Turks in Istanbul, in which the Irish supporters were attacked before, during and after the match. Friends of mine said they were lucky to get out of there alive; an experience I went through myself later in Turkey and Nigeria.

And so it was full steam ahead for the 1994 World Cup in the USA. Our first match of the campaign was held in Dublin in May 1992 where we faced Albania. We won 2–0. Our streak continued with a 4–0 win over Latvia, a new country, in Dublin. We then travelled back to Copenhagen and Seville to play Denmark and Spain and got two good nil-all draws. A particularly hostile match against Northern Ireland took place in Dublin in March 1993, but we won 3–0, and followed this with a 1–1 draw against Denmark. I didn't get to the game against Albania, but our team secured another three points with a 2–1 victory.

One of the best trips I was on was in June 1993, when we set out for the two away games in Latvia and Lithuania. We set out from Cork at 3 a.m. on a Monday morning to catch our flight to Moscow. Brendan, my son, who was twelve at the time, joined us on this never to be forgotten trip. The flight to Moscow was uneventful and when we arrived at our hotel we went straight down to dinner. I think it was duck that was served, but there was not very much of it there, so we all tried the McDonalds which had opened a month before. To us, the prices were very cheap at £1 for a Big Mac Meal, but they were too expensive for the Russians, so we saw a lot of begging outside the premises. It has changed a lot since then.

When we got back to the hotel Brendan decided to go to bed. I said I would be up after him but when I did, ten minutes later, I couldn't get into the room as he had locked the door. I banged and banged on the door and telephoned the room, but he was fast asleep. Eventually a maintenance man had to come and take the door off the hinges to let me in.

Next day we headed to the main railway station, upgraded our train tickets to first class for $3 and headed on the sixteen-hour, 500km train journey to Riga. It was lovely going through the countryside, though at times the train went so slow that you could get out and walk alongside it. There are four classes on the train in Russia: first class luxury, where you had bunks and a Burko boiler with hot water; second class with seats; third class with planks and fourth class with no seats or planks, just floor space. We were lucky as we were in first class and we each had a bunk. Being cute Cork and Limerick men we brought a lot of milk for the journey and enjoyed decent cups of tea as we travelled through the dramatic scenery of the countryside.

At the time, the Baltic states were just coming to terms with their independence. When you arrived at the border, the Russian soldiers came on the train and checked everyone, passports, etc. Then the train would move 100 yards and the same procedure happened on the other side of the border. We could see that those with inadequate documentation were removed from the train on both sides.

Riga was a beautiful city and we settled easily into our accommodation, a former mental hospital – we felt quite at home there! It was a worthwhile trip as Ireland won the match handy at 2–0.

On our way to Vilnius we criss-crossed a number of Baltic states. We were in a convoy of buses and we all stopped out in the middle of the country at a local shop to buy water and soft drinks. All we had were US dollars and they didn't know what currency it was so they refused to take it. If only they knew, they could have retired after what we would have paid them. We also stopped at a railway station where I soon smelled food. I found the restaurant and in we went and had a look at what the natives were eating. I made a gesture to one of the ladies and ordered steak for the thirteen of us. It was delicious and even more so as when the bill came it amounted to approx 50p each. Except for two of the party we gave them extra money and the hugs and kisses we got were worth it. I discovered that we had given them a tip equivalent to a month's wages each. It was great to see their happy faces.

Our next port of call was St Petersburg with its dramatic architecture, vast squares and museums – very impressive. We stayed here for a day or two. One day as we were walking down a side street I saw a name up over a shop that caught my eye; it looked familiar even though it was in Russian. We went in and discovered that it was a bookies owned by Liam Cashman, a bookmaker from Cork who was trying to show the Russians how to gamble and hopefully lose some money.

The Sunday was the anniversary of my brother Mick's ordination and the people of his parish in Knockavilla, near Bandon, Co. Cork, were having the celebration that Mick had planned before he died, so we decided we would do something as well. As we walked down the street in St Petersburg, Jerry Mackey spotted a church and we went in. It was a Russian Orthodox church in very bad repair, and the 'parish priest' was selling candles. We gave him some dollars, lit some candles and said a few prayers.

One night we found ourselves in the hotel early and were having a chat and a few drinks, when Brendan said he was going up to the room for a few minutes, probably to watch television. After ten minutes or so he came back, pointing to another Irish guy saying, 'she didn't keep him too long'. I asked what he meant and he said that when he was going up to the room, the same guy and a 'lady of the night' were in the lift with him and went into a room down the corridor from our room. He may have left Ireland a twelve-year-old boy, but he came back more like a twenty-five-year-old man.

While in St Petersburg we went to the state circus – a truly magnificent spectacle. It is one of the leading circuses of the country, held in a stone building, said to be one of the most beautiful circus buildings in Europe. We also visited Minsk in Belarus which is the city nearest Chernobyl, where I had one of the nicest meals ever in a state palace.

Vilnius is another beautiful city just getting used to independence. Two places of note were the beautiful cathedral where Pope John Paul II said mass on his visit, and the television tower which the locals protected against the Russian army by forming a human chain around it; the view for the top is magnificent and you can see the whole city.

The one characteristic I found in all these states was that they had wanted independence but now they had it, it was making their lives miserable as they had to fend for themselves. Up to then the Russian state had catered for all their needs, but now you had the situation where those who could not find work had to beg to survive.

We beat the Lithuanians 1–0 and left for Moscow on another slow train. There was confusion on the train as we discovered that the travel agent was trying to pull a fast one by saying that our scheduled flight to Shannon would not be going and instead we would have to fly to Dublin later that night. We arrived in Moscow and some of us decided to go straight to the airport, as I knew that all Aeroflot flights to the west stopped in Shannon. We nearly caused a riot at the taxi stand as they all wanted to take us to the airport for dollars. On arrival in Moscow Airport, with gestures and nods we communicated sufficiently and were issued with tickets for the first flight to Shannon. We christened ourselves the Moscow Eleven as only eleven of us went to the airport. The others didn't care if they went to Dublin. The worst that could have happened was that we would be refused tickets and would have to wait for the others and fly to Dublin.

The security in Moscow Airport was severe and we had to go through at least ten checkpoints and searches before we got on the plane – but not before I bought a bottle of Champagne. Even after all the checkpoints, as we sat on the plane waiting for take-off the police still came on board and took a number of people off the flight. We don't know why they were removed, but they did it in quite a threatening way and we were glad we weren't them. Perhaps Siberia was their final destination!

The flight back home was uneventful, except for a big Russian who kept telling us how rich he was and that he was going to Cuba on holidays. He was looking down his nose at us wearing our tracksuits and wanted to know where we were going. I told him 'Shannon Airport, in Ireland', and asked him whether he was getting off the plane there.

'No,' he replied. 'We are not allowed off the plane in case we would defect.'

'Did you every hear of Cunta Cinte?' I asked.

He said he had, on television, so I said, 'I am like him,

Top: lighting candles in the church; middle: Brendan asleep on the train; bottom: the entrance to Lenin's tomb

a free man, I can get off in Shannon.' That shut him up for the remainder of the flight.

I had been invited to a wedding that day and I said I would call to the church on the way from the airport, so Brendan, Jerry and I stood at the back of the church unshaven and in our three-day-old tracksuits. As the bride and groom, Tessa and Barry, came down the aisle, I presented them with the bottle of Champagne I had bought in Moscow Airport.

Our next two games in the group were against Lithuania in Dublin, which we won 2–0, and against Spain in Dublin, which we lost 3–1. So all was set up for the last game of the group in Belfast on 16 November 1993 where we needed at least a draw to qualify for USA 1994. I was finding it very hard to get a ticket for the match but I was determined to be there. My usual contact for tickets, the late Donie Forde, was unable to secure a ticket for me as the FAI and IFA had made an agreement to have no travelling supporters. However, later Donie gave me his own ticket and I arrived in Dublin by car and took the twenty-minute flight to Belfast.

The atmosphere was hostile to say the least. I walked around Windsor Park and bought twenty-five programmes for all those who couldn't make the trip. I felt fairly intimidated by the Northern Ireland supporters who had an aggressive manner. The tension was palpable. This was the game where the Northern Ireland manager, Bill Bingham, is alleged to have made a gesture to our fans. I didn't see it, so cannot comment on it. The tension was electric

With John Aldridge in Aldergrove Airport in Belfast

as the North took the lead and it looked as if our dream was over until Alan McLoughlin cropped up and scored a scorcher of a goal. The game ended in a 1–1 draw. This was great, but we now had to wait to see if Spain got the result they wanted in Seville as we would only get through if they didn't. Word came through on the RTÉ monitor that they hadn't achieved it and the celebrations started inside the very hostile Windsor Park. At one stage I needed to go to the toilet but decided to hold on as there was a very vicious crowd around and I felt it would be safer later.

After the match we were herded like sheep to waiting buses and escorted out of the grounds by the British army and RUC to the safety of Aldergrove Airport, where we waited the arrival of the team. They duly arrived and we began a small party, where I tried unsuccessfully to get a photograph of the four Cork people, Denis Irwin, Brian Carey, myself and a guy from Mayfield by the name of Roy Keane. Instead, I got a photo of John Aldridge and me. The party in Belfast was nothing to the reception awaiting us in Dublin Airport. The flight was delayed as there were so many people gathering in Dublin Airport and they were trying to avoid chaos. It is estimated that up to 10,000 people gathered there.

It was a wonderful sight to walk down the steps of the plane and see all the people gathered to welcome us home from a hundred miles up the road. The party went on late into the night and it was 4 a.m. when I finally sat into my car to head to Cork. I could hardly remember any of the journey home I was on such a high.

– 20 –

USA, 1994

Italy in New Jersey, Mexico in Orlando, Norway in New Jersey: this was the schedule for Ireland's first games in the 1994 World Cup. We set out from Shannon to JFK airport with no accommodation organised. I saw a hotel booking office in the airport and went over to see if I could organise some rooms. It turned out that a Donegal man had a hotel in the Queen's district of New York with some rooms still available and also had a courtesy bus which would take us there. They neglected to tell us that there was a train strike in Queen's so the only way out of the area was by taxi. We settled on a stretch limo to take us to Giant's Stadium, which the Donegal man also arranged. And what a sight that stadium was. A three-tier, circular, open space completely full of masses of green and blue jerseys.

The Italians did not know what hit them. They didn't realise that there were so many Irish living in the US, or that so many Irish travelled there for the games. Even in the fierce heat that day, the stadium was electric. Our tickets were up high and we had the best view ever. It was the first time I saw escalators in a sports stadium.

The atmosphere became even better when the great man himself, Ray Houghton, popped up to get a great goal from over thirty yards out. Stuttgart revisited, but not for long. The team played out of their skins to rattle the Italians and gain revenge for Rome four years before. They got us the best possible start with a 1–0 victory and the party continued long into the night. On the way back from the stadium we got a little lost and ended up in JFK Airport. We were fortunate to be able to call the hotel's courtesy bus to bring us back to the hotel.

The next day we did the tourist things around Queen's and New York, but we hardly noticed the sights as we were full of anticipation about the rest of our trip. When booking the transatlantic part of our ticket, I had discovered that you could book internal flights a lot cheaper from Ireland as part of the deal, but you had to book them in groups of 1, 3, 5, 7, etc. We decided to go for the three-flight package and go to Nassau in the Bahamas on the Sunday morning. We headed to JFK and flew to Philadelphia. The ten of us had the plane to ourselves to Miami, with a brief stopover, then changed planes and flew on to Nassau. This was considered one flight.

On arrival at Nassau Airport, we had to book hotel rooms before being allowed into the country. When that was sorted, we headed to our hotel: all our rooms were surrounding the swimming pool and across the road was the Caribbean Sea and beautiful sandy beaches. We had fallen on our feet and stayed there for three days. Before we left some of us decided that we could retire permanently to the Bahamas as we would love to end our days there. The pace of life is slow, with nobody in a hurry as there is nowhere to go. That applies to services too: one night we went for dinner and it took one and a half hours before I got my meal. The staff would disappear for a while and then resume serving.

After our wonderful few days, we headed back to Miami on part two of our three-flight package, where we were met by a few more of our party who had gone to different places in the States. We hired an eight-seater van and drove off to Orlando to find a house I had rented before we left Ireland. Eventually we located the house which was an ordinary bungalow with four or five rooms and an indoor swimming pool – heaven, and a great base for the week.

Orlando is a really commercial city and everywhere you go you are reminded that they want your money. We did all the usual trips to Disney World and Water World but found the heat overpowering. It didn't take us long to discover that the trick was to put half a bottle of water in the freezer overnight, top it up in the morning, and keep it with you in your backpack. You could top it up during the day from water taps around the place and it kept you nice and cool.

To get value for money in Disney World and to see as much as you could you had to be there early. We were there from nine in the morning till ten at night and by then our bodies were totally wrecked.

I really wanted to see a space shuttle. We had been on a simulated one, but I wanted to see the real thing, and to visit Cape Canaveral. Six of us decided to go there and, as it happened, I knew a priest from Kilkenny, Willie Hennessy, who was doing some parish work out there for the summer, so we called to him. Willie used to exchange with another priest every year for the summer – a great arrangement – and Willie was quite happy out in that heat for three months every year.

We arrived at Cape Canaveral and went on the tour but I was so tired that I slept on the bus for most of it. It became a great source of amusement as I had pestered the others so much about wanting to see the space shuttle base and then I slept through most of the tour. However, I still managed to see the space shuttles themselves and it was fascinating to see them up close and celebrate the history of their landing on the moon.

The match in Orlando against Mexico was fixed for midday, when the sun was at its highest. We arrived at the stadium early but even walking around was difficult in the heat. However, there was great craic and again the paddies were on their best behaviour. The timing of the game was definitely in favour of the Mexicans who would be used to this heat and we lost 2–1. Our boys were drained as were the supporters but we needed to recover quickly as we had another game to attend early the next morning: a pub was found in downtown Orlando, which was showing the Munster football final between Cork and Kerry. There was great colour in the pub between the Cork and Kerry jerseys and great banter as always.

We really enjoyed our stay in Orlando and before we

left decided we should go to a jeans factory outlet. We found it but each time we crossed the road to get near it, it seemed to get farther away. We couldn't find the entrance. At one stage we drove about fifteen miles beyond it, turned back but still couldn't find it. Eventually there was nothing for it but to do an illegal turn on the highway, cross over the oncoming traffic and drive into the factory. I perfected this manoeuvre at a later stage in Japan.

We then flew to Newark airport and back to the Sunset Hotel in Queen's. At that stage the strike was over, so we were able to get trains in and out of Queen's. New York was busy at the time because the Gay Olympics were on. We met some of the competitors on the train one day and found them fascinating. There was a lot of pink worn on that train.

The match in Giants Stadium on 28 June was against Norway. Again, a huge Irish contingent turned up to cheer on the boys in green, on another warm day. The match itself ended in a nil-all draw and that somehow or another guaranteed that the four teams in our group got into phase two.

We were drawn to play Holland, again, in Orlando, six days later. As we were due to fly home the next day, a decision had to be made. Aer Lingus didn't help. They wanted $500 to change the ticket and another $500 to fly down to Orlando. We decided to come home and that I would try and get out again. In JFK we were kept waiting in the plane as Air Force 1, the president's plane, was supposed to be landing and nothing moves while that is around. Unfortunately we didn't get to see it.

We landed in Shannon and straight away I rang my travel agent in Cork, who had always been very good to me and tried to get me back to the States again. There was one seat out of Manchester to Orlando, but by the time I got to Cork, after I stopped for a quick snooze in the car outside of Limerick, that seat was gone. Over the next few days I tried everywhere to get out but to no avail. I eventually had to settle with watching the game on television.

I wasn't going to get caught again, so I booked a flight to Dallas and then onto Los Angeles as these were two of the venues we would be playing in if we beat Holland. But it wasn't to be and the Dutch once more ended our dreams of progressing in a major tournament. I didn't need to pay for these flights ahead of time, which was one of the benefits of the travel agent system.

– 21 –

Euro '96

After the disappointment of the USA, it was onto the start of the campaign for Euro '96. Our first match was a 3–0 win over Latvia in Riga followed by a 4–0 win at home over Liechtenstein in Dublin. Our next match was against Northern Ireland in Belfast in November 1994. Tony and I set off on the Monday, with the intention of first going to Newcastle for an under-21 match against England. We intended to stay in Larne on Monday night but caught the ferry and instead stayed in Stranraer. The following morning we headed off for a three-hour drive to Newcastle, arriving outside the stadium at 2 p.m. for an 8 p.m. kick-off. As Tony is a shopaholic, we filled in the time by going into the city. We eventually got back to the stadium to discover that the match was a sell-out (30,000 at an under-21 when a good game would usually generate 5,000) which had never been heard of. After a struggle and a bit of grovelling we got two tickets at the end of the stand. It was a great game and ended in a 1–1 draw.

After the game we went back to the car only to find that it would not start. One of the heater plugs had died.

We had to get a push to start the car but we had to wait until all the traffic was gone. Eventually we got going and headed back to Stranraer, hungry and tired. It was just as well the car knew the way as the driver had a very hard time trying to stay awake. But for Tony we would never have made it; we drove into Stranraer and at about 4 a.m. found our B&B.

The next day we got an early ferry back to Larne and did a little tour of Belfast. The match itself was uneventful and we won 4–0. After the match we met a few guys who asked us where our car was and we told them it was near Windsor Park. They said they would come with us as it was a tough area. We found the car intact and headed back to the B&B. The next morning we went into Larne RUC station where we got a great reception and were shown around. One of the lads asked me would the gardaí support a movement which the RUC called PAP. I said I would see what I could do for him, but I needed to know what PAP stood for. 'Police Against Peace', he said, as since the ceasefire most of their overtime had been cut!

Tony and I left Larne and headed south after some shopping in Newry. As a shopkeeper, Tony always had an eye for the bargain.

Ireland's next match was a 'friendly' against England in February 1995 in Lansdowne Road. This was always going to be a high-risk game for the organisers and so it proved to be. I took Brendan and my nephew, Barry, to the game. They were both about fourteen at the time but I could only get tickets for them in the East stand while mine was at the far end of the stand, away from trouble. The English supporters ran riot and the match had to be postponed.

There was no point in staying as it didn't look like it was going to continue that day and, in any case, my concern was for Brendan and Barry. I waited at a pre-arranged point and after about half an hour of anxiety, the two lads appeared, as cool as cucumbers, having had a great view of the riot. It was a disgraceful display that had no place in sport.

The following month another potentially explosive game took place in Lansdowne Road. This was the return game against the North, but thankfully it passed off without incident with an honourable 1–1 draw. This was followed by a 1–0 win over Portugal in Dublin.

Our next trip was into the unknown. Atlases were scoured to find out where Liechtenstein was, and eventually we located the small principality stuck between Austria, Switzerland and Germany. We decided to go on a day trip out of Dublin. Jessy, Jerry and I set out from Cork on Friday evening, booked into our B&B in Dublin and early next day took a flight to Zurich. There we were bussed to Vaduz, the capital of Liechtenstein, which consists of a main street and a castle and, of course, an Irish bar.

We had something to eat in the bar and overheard two visitors saying it was also a post office. When they asked the proprietor of the bar how much it would cost to post two cards to Ireland, she did not know where Ireland was and had to ask someone if it was in Europe or the USA.

The setting for the match was spectacular: the pitch was placed in a valley with a mountain as a backdrop behind one of the goals. If only the match had been as spectacular, but it ended in a nil-all draw in a game we should have won easily.

After the match we were bussed back to Zurich Airport where we boarded our flight and taxied down the runway. However, the pilot announced that he was being refused permission to take off as we were a minute late and the airport closes to all traffic at 10 p.m. It was 9.58 and we would not be clear of the airport in time. We had to disembark. There were no travel reps, no shops, no coffee shops open; all we could do was sit in the airport for the night and bitch about our misfortune and anyone who might have caused it.

At 6 a.m. on the Sunday morning, we boarded again and took off for Dublin, cold and hungry. We were given the dinner from the night before which at least was still hot. We arrived in Dublin and went to the B&B and explained our case, but the woman demanded the money for the night we had missed. I had recommended a lot of people to this B&B, so needless to say I didn't recommend it again.

As we left Dublin our next port of call was Limerick for the Munster hurling semi-final, Cork v Clare. Everything was going great for Cork until a certain Ollie Baker stuck his nose in and had to get a last minute goal for Clare to make them the winners. It was a bad weekend for us and started the Banner on their rollercoaster to a glorious period in Irish hurling history. This dispelled the myth that Biddy Earley had put a curse on Clare winning an All-Ireland.

Tony O'Sullivan, myself, Mairéad O'Callaghan and Gary Spain in Lisbon

The next two games in the group were home and away to Austria with two 3–1 defeats. We went on a day trip again to Vienna, a beautiful city. On this trip I lost my precious scarf which I had for over twenty years; a sad day both on and off the field. The team then got back on track with a 2–1 win over Latvia in Dublin.

We all headed to Faro in Portugal in November for the return match and the last one of the group. Our stay in

Praia de Rocha was pleasant but the place was saturated with noisy paddies and a constant buzz of noise. We hired a car and headed off to get the under-21 game about 100 miles north of Lisbon. Crossing the Vasco da Gama bridge into Lisbon is some experience; at 17.2km long it's the longest bridge in Europe.

After the under-21 game we returned to Lisbon for the game on the Wednesday night. On the way we saw a sign for Fatima and diverted there. It was a lovely place to visit: a huge open area surrounded by impressive basilicas and churches. One of the sights was a man walking on his knees across this vast area, having obviously travelled much further with someone who seemed to be his wife standing over him with an umbrella. We wondered what he had done to deserve this penance. Whatever happened to a simple 'three Hail Marys'?

On our arrival in Lisbon we found our hotel and decided we would walk or get a bus to the stadium. We were lucky that we left early, as we usually do, as we like to have plenty time to look around the stadia. This time we went to the wrong stadium and we had to dash to the other one to be in time for the game. It rained most of the evening, which is unusual down south in Faro.

As the match progressed the rain got worse and we were all soaked; on the continent most of the stadiums are open. We lost 3–0, but at least we had made it to the play-offs. Once again we were drawn against Holland in Liverpool. A huge Irish contingent arrived at Anfield, but the Dutch once more got the better of us. Euro '96 was not to be.

A glorious era in Irish soccer came to an end when Jack Charlton resigned having led us to one Euro final and two World Cup finals.

The next man to become manager was Mick McCarthy who, as Captain Fantastic, had already led Ireland to two World Cups. His first match in charge was a friendly against Russia, which we lost 2–0. This was followed by an away loss to the Czech Republic and then a home loss to Portugal. A bad start, though all of the games were friendlies. In fact, McCarthy's first eight games in charge were all friendlies, including three in the states against USA, Mexico and Bolivia. I had intended going to this tournament in the States but others had different ideas and I found myself in Dromad, Co. Louth doing a tour of duty over the outbreak of BSE.

– 22 –

World Cup '98

The draw for the 1998 World Cup put us in the group with Liechtenstein, Iceland, Romania, Macedonia and Lithuania. We started well and in the first three matches we beat Liechtenstein and Macedonia in Dublin and also drew with Iceland.

I was supposed to go to Skopje for the game against Macedonia, but due to the war in this area found it hard to get flights which were all cancelled at the last minute. Our next match was an away trip to Bucharest for the match against Romania. Brendan, Tony and I decided we would go there on a one-day trip. As in most of these countries you have to have an entry visa so we sent away our passports to the Romanian embassy in Dublin to get them. On the Monday the embassy phoned me and told me that Tony's and my passports were out of date, but Brendan's was okay. We left Cork at 4 a.m. on Tuesday to go and pick up our passports from the embassy. We got all the forms and photographs stamped for the new application and headed for Dublin.

I had made contact with a lovely lady in the passport

office who agreed to look after us, which was a great help. We eventually got our new passports and had to head back to the embassy before it closed to get the visa. In the end it worked out fine. We met Brendan off the train and headed to our hotel to sleep as we had a 4 a.m. start again the next morning.

It always amazes me how the Irish drink their way to a match. They start in the airport, then on the plane and once they arrive in the strange city the first thing they look for is an Irish bar. On this trip we were taken to a native restaurant and bar where the food and drink was cheap and tasty, but, though they were only five hours away from Ireland, the others just wanted an Irish pub and its inflated prices. In the Irish pub they were charged $5 for a pint of Guinness, but next door in the Romanian pub they could have got a pint of beer for fifty cent.

Tony, Brendan and I went for a quick tour of Bucharest and did a little bit of cheap shopping. The match was disappointing as we lost 1–0 and so we arrived back in Dublin at some unearthly hour and drove back next day to Cork.

The next two games we beat Liechtenstein and drew with Lithuania. Then came the away trips to Iceland and Lithuania. I was not able to go to either of these and didn't even get to see the game in Reykjavik as I was stuck at a messy domestic at work and had to try to see bits of the game on television in between trying to restore peace. The domestic lasted the full length of the game. It was as though the couple knew I wanted to see the match and kept up the argument until the game was over.

Our last match was against Romania. They had the great Hagi on their team and we could only manage a draw. We were back to the play-offs. Again, this was a home and away game against Belgium. The first game in Dublin ended in a 1–1 draw and two weeks later we headed off to Brussels, full of expectations for the return leg. It wasn't to be. Once more we were the bridesmaids, not the bride, and had to settle for watching and thinking what might have been if we had got to the World Cup in France.

And so it was time for the usual round of friendlies before the next campaign: Euro 2000. In this group we had some interesting countries such as Croatia, Macedonia and Yugoslavia, who were all at war with each other, and we also had Malta.

Our first game in Dublin saw us gain victories against Croatia and Malta. Then came our visit to Belgrade in November 1998. We were all advised not to go as it was not safe and there was a rumour going around that NATO forces were going to bomb Belgrade. The claim was denied so we decided to go.

Belgrade was a real old Soviet-looking city, with huge, grey, drab buildings. Our hotel, Hotel M, was up the road from the Red Star Belgrade stadium where the match was played. It was later used as a refugee camp when the city was bombed. Even though we were in the middle of a war, I never felt in any danger as a semi-truce had been called. People would not accept Visa cards as these were American, yet they loved to get dollars. Our hotel was a long walk from the bus terminal which used to get us into the city centre and all along the pavement people were selling petrol from cans. Where they got it from, I don't know.

The atmosphere in the stadium was tense, but we got a great welcome from the Yugoslavian fans. I think they appreciated the fact that the few hundred of us had risked travelling. But there were a number of surprises in store for us: one was the fact that while the admission to the ground for the native was the equivalent of about 50c, we were charged about $20, with the FAI and the travel agents adding on a profit for themselves. It's still cheaper that going to a game in Lansdowne Road though. We went down 1–0 in this match, even though we played well and deserved to score.

The next surprise awaiting us the next morning was that we would have to pay a $20 'tax' to get out of the country. When we all challenged this it was raised to $40. We paid the first $20 but refused the additional $20. As we all sat in the plane on the runway we were told that we were not moving until everyone, including the pilot and crew, paid. We eventually all paid up. Luckily some people had extra money and were able to pay for those who had spent everything. Again, they would not accept their own money, it had to be US dollars. We later learned that the second $20 was for the team plane, which had left the night before. They had refused to pay the money and, rather than cause an international incident with FIFA, they let the team go and caught the supporters. We were assured that the FAI would reimburse us.

The 1995 ill-fated match against England in Lansdowne Road was another where we should have been reimbursed for a match that was abandoned. In this match the English supporters ran riot and the game had to be abandoned. While we didn't get our money back for the game, the English supporters got more than they bargained for from a well-prepared garda force who got on top of the situation and did us proud.

– 23 –

The Under-20 Soccer World Cup

The year 1999 was a very busy one, travel-wise and sports-wise. I had been appointed as a selector for the Watergrasshill hurling team and we played twenty-five matches – most of which I managed to attend – as well as numerous training sessions. Our team won the league and championship double, which was a nice achievement, and I still managed to get a lot of travelling to places such as Lagos, Ibaden and Kano in Nigeria; Zagreb in Croatia; Valetta in Malta; Skopje in Macedonia; and Burza in Turkey.

Tony O'Sullivan and I decided that we would go to Nigeria for the under-20 World Cup. As it happened, my niece, Deirdre, was working with Irish Aid in the region and I made contact with her. Her office was attached to the Irish embassy in Lagos and they had a big involvement as Ireland was playing. When travelling to Nigeria you need to get an entry visa, and to get that, you need an invitation from someone living in Nigeria, which was handy for me with Deirdre there. She could fax the necessary documents to the Nigerian embassy in Dublin. Tony's application was accepted but mine could not be issued as Deirdre had invited 'Jim' Ryan and 'James' Ryan was the name on the passport. I had to repeat the whole procedure and ended up going to Dublin to pick up the passports.

We headed off from Cork to Amsterdam on the first leg of our journey in early April 1999. From there we got a direct flight with KLM to Lagos. On the way we met up with a few English blokes who were working on the oil-rigs in Nigeria. They knew their way through Lagos Airport – with a few dollars here and there – and in no time we were gone through customs. All the workers in the airport seemed to be carrying carpet around with them and, at a moment's notice, they would drop to the floor and start praying.

The first thing to hit you when you leave the terminal building at Lagos Airport is the immense heat and humidity. Just standing, my shirt was dripping wet. We had been booked into a B&B and that night we found it hard to sleep, even with the air-conditioning, but we wouldn't have been able to sleep at all without it. We went down for breakfast the next morning and afterwards went to pay our bill: it came to $125 each and $20 for breakfast. We got out of there as fast as we could. We went to the Irish embassy to see if we could get cheaper accommodation as we had an apartment booked which would not be ready for a few days. This was Holy Thursday and, as luck would have it, we met a few Irish nuns who on seeing our plight, offered us a room in their convent for a few days in a very poor part of Lagos. As is customary with us when we are on a long stay, Tony brings vacuum-packed sausages, rashers and puddings, so when we arrived at the convent, we presented some to the nuns to eat after Easter. There is always a problem with their electricity supply and it can go off at the spur of the moment so we were glad to share the breakfast and enjoy it while it was still chilled and safe to eat.

We went with the nuns, two Irish and one Indian, to the Easter ceremonies in an open-air church in the poorest part of Lagos, where open sewers are part of the infrastructure. On arrival at the church one of the nuns took us to meet the priest, a newly-ordained Nigerian man. She said I was the assistant manager of the Irish football team and that Tony was the team doctor. He was very impressed to have such VIPs in his congregation. When he came to the altar he said he had two very important people here and to give us a big round of applause, which they did. I said to Tony that in this heat and humidity, we had better pray that nobody would collapse and need a doctor.

The ceremonies took three hours, during which the priest had everyone singing, dancing and giving their money. He told them they were not giving enough to the collection for retired priests (Peter's Pence Collection) – I called it the pope's drinking money. I thought it was unfair to give out to them as, being in a really poor part of Lagos, they hadn't a bubble. He made each one of them in turn go up to the altar and show what they were putting into the collection box. We made our way back to the convent through the dimly lit streets. Just as we sat down to supper the power went out, so we had a lovely candle lit supper on Holy Thursday.

On Friday morning, I awoke to the beautiful smell of an Irish fry. I went up to the kitchen to remind the nuns what day it was, Good Friday, and that meat was forbidden. They said that when you get food like this out here, Good Friday doesn't count. On top of that, the Indian nun, who didn't eat pork, was told by the others that there was no meat in the black pudding so she had a piece of everything. It was one of the best meals I have ever had. The nuns told us there was no need for us to go to the ceremonies at midday, which were to start with the Stations of the Cross, as they normally took three hours and that we would be in plenty of time going at 3 p.m. They were not going either, so we arranged to meet up at 2.30 p.m. The ceremonies finally finished at 6.30 p.m. – which meant six and a half hours in 100°F heat and 100°F humidity. I don't think he would get away with that in Ireland.

Next morning we left the convent and headed to the embassy again to get a lift to Ibadan, approximately 100 miles north of Lagos, on one of the most dangerous roads anywhere. The police had not been paid for a while and we had a few of them with us. It was rumoured that some of them used to do armed robberies in their spare time and it was not safe to travel after dark.

We arrived in Ibadan with nowhere to stay but the SMA Fathers put us up in their compound. There we met a great Corkman, Martin O'Farrell, SMA, and Peter McCawville, a native of Tyrone and the PRO of the SMA. Martin offered us accommodation and warned us about the lizards and various flying insects. We had all got the necessary injections and had a multitude of spray repellents, which kept them at bay.

Tony and myself in Ibadan

The first match was against Mexico, and the Nigerians were full of expectation. There were thousands outside the stadium who could not afford the admission charge and inside it was empty. Sepp Blatter, the president of FIFA, was to attend the match with a view to Nigeria hosting the 2006 World Cup. Everything was in order except someone forgot to bribe the man in charge of the electrical power and he turned the lights off after twenty minutes of the game. Any plans for Nigeria hosting the game in 2006 went out with that light.

The heat and humidity were awful for us sitting in the stand, so how the players coped is beyond me. After the game Tony and I attended a reception for the team in their hotel and we got a great welcome as we were the only two travelling fans. Davy Keogh's banner was seen on television at most matches, but there was no sign of it or him here. The manager, Brian Kerr, and his assistant, Noel O'Reilly, made us feel like part of the set-up, as did all the players, such as Robbie Keane, Stephen McPhail, Richie Baker, Damien Duff and a good Corkman, Colin Healy from Ballincollig, who was delighted with all the Cork people around.

Also there was the Irish ambassador to Nigeria, Joe Lynch. I later presented a Watergrasshill hurling tie to him and to Brian Kerr. During my chairmanship of the club it was agreed to have a club tie which had the crest of the GAA and Watergrasshill in Irish around it. When I got them made however, most of the members would not take them, I don't know why, so I have given them to ambassadors and heads of state around the world. I am hopeful that one day one of them will appear on television wearing one of these ties.

At the reception we also met the Irish press who were covering the games for the Irish newspapers. These included Karl MacGinty, *Irish Independent*; Emmet Malone, *Irish Times*; Noel Spillane, *Cork Examiner*; David McKenzie, *Sunday Tribune*; Damien Lawlor, *The Star*; Paul Buttner, freelance; and photographers Dave Maher and Lorraine O'Sullivan. Even though we had lost 1–0 to Mexico – once the lights were turned back on – there was still a good atmosphere in the hotel, where Mexico, Saudi Arabia and Australia, the other three teams in our group, were also staying. The Irish party went on for a while and there was a great sing-song with the team and a number of priests and nuns. Tony and I went back to the SMA seminary and talked with the priests until the early hours about our travels and sporting obsessions. They were intrigued.

Over the course of that trip we had many deep and interesting conversations with the priests and nuns. It is only when you are in their midst that you realise the sacrifices they make to bring religion to the people. You can also see how they love the laid back lifestyle – if you can't do it today, sure tomorrow is coming. It was during one of our conversations that I came across two wonderful sayings, the first one: 'If we had afterthoughts beforehand wouldn't life be so much easier', and 'A committee is a group of people who individually can do nothing but collectively can meet and decide that nothing can be done'. I thought these were so true of Irish thinking.

The priests were very good to us and showed us all around the area. Anytime a priest is driving or travelling around out there, he wears a white robe, as do all religious people. Bandits are not inclined to rob the religious for fear of reprisals from the Lord. We were more worried about the potholes which are like nothing you would see in Ireland – they were craters.

Next morning, we were collected by our armed bus and headed to our apartment in Lagos. As it was not safe to go out at night in Lagos, we stayed in the apartment, which was in a protected compound. We got a loan of a television set and settled down to watch some of the other games in the tournament. The commentator would start off full of enthusiasm and after a while would go silent and we were left watching a game with no commentary. All you could hear was chat in the background or cups being hit off something. The commentator would come back for a while and get all excited before disappearing again.

We had a lovely lady who used to clean the apartment every day. She cleaned with a child wrapped around her, perfectly happy. We went shopping with her once to buy water and groceries. We tried to carry the water to help her but she insisted in taking the fifteen-litre drums on her head. I tried this balancing act, but could not do it.

We returned to Ibadan for the second match, against Saudi Arabia, and won that game 2–0. Again it struck me that we were passing thousands who could not afford to go into Liberty Stadium and still the stadium was nearly empty. Surely it would have been better to fill the stadium and create a better atmosphere. The game was shown live across the world and it was clear there was no excitement.

We were invited to take part in the daily mass for the team in their hotel, which was concelebrated by the priests from Challenge SMA House. The players took a shine to one of the priests, Frank Diamond, as he was just a year or two older than them and not long ordained.

One of the days we stayed in Challenge there was a wedding, which we were invited to attend in our Irish jerseys. The bride and groom arrived with their five children, in magnificent colour. Before they went up the aisle, the priest, Ali Kelly, asked them had they been to confession, as they had to be in the state of grace before they received the sacrament. They were reluctant to do this, for their own reasons, but they had no other choice and off they went to confession and returned full of grace. It was a wonderful ceremony but we had to leave before it ended as it was going on for hours.

Almost every international football match that Ireland plays involved an amateur 'international' taking place in the lead up. In this case it was the Irish media, accompanied by Fr Frank Diamond and Fr Peter McCawville, against a team of local footballers. Hundreds turned up to watch the game on a back patch near Liberty Stadium and the Irish won 3–0. After the game the journalists were invited back to the SMA house for a meal and we all had a wonderful night. It was great for them to get out of the hotel as there was no such thing as going for a walk in downtown Ibadan.

The phone system in Nigeria was nearly non-existent, worse than Ireland in the 1950s, and very expensive. The journalists were very frustrated with the system, trying to get scripts back to their offices in Ireland to meet deadlines. One of the reporters got his copy away, but when it appeared on the paper it made Fr Frank Diamond sound like Fr Dougal from *Fr Ted* – a little scatty and unconventional – which in fact he wasn't. This was not received well and Brian Kerr placed a ban on that reporter so none of the players would talk to him. In fact one night we were all invited to a party at the Guinness brewery in Ibadan and word was left that he was not to be let in. Nigeria can be a very lonely place when you are an outcast. In fairness to the reporter he may have written a nice piece, but sub-editors may have decided to make a 'better' story out of it.

The last match in the group was against Australia on the Saturday. On our way to the match there were mile-long queues for petrol, which was crazy when you consider that Nigeria is an oil-rich nation yet their own people cannot get easy access to it. I heard that 5% of people there have 95% of the wealth. At one stage in the 1980s, Nigeria was in the top ten richest countries in the world, but by 1999 it was in the bottom ten.

Ireland needed at least a draw with Australia to get into phase two, the quarter finals, and this they did with a 4–0 victory over a fancied Aussie team. After the game and celebrations on the field in which the Irish team were joined by hundreds of Nigerians in the sweltering heat, we all headed to the team hotel again for a victory celebration. We were joined by the other three teams who were fascinated with the way the Irish could party. We were now in the quarter finals of the World Cup and were to play the hosts, Nigeria, in the northern town of Kano. How the hell were we to get up there?

As the night of celebrations went on and the team

drifted away to bed, the rest of us headed back to the SMA house where the conversation continued on into the night. One of the stories was of a priest saying mass one day when he asked one of the local chiefs to give a blessing. The chief started his prayers and sermon, the priest went out and had his dinner, then a siesta and a swim and when he came back the chief was still in full flight. I could well believe it.

One day when we were in Ibadan, Tony and I were taken by Peter and Martin to meet the local archbishop who was very impressed with us and our sense of adventure. He had been to Ireland and said he liked it very much. We were told that he was being tipped as the first black pope, his name is Archbishop Job (pronounced Jobe), and we wait with interest.

We returned to our apartment in Lagos and arranged a flight through the embassy staff to Kano, 500 miles north, on the Wednesday morning. Deirdre had a hotel room arranged – the advantage of having good nieces. We flew with KABO Air, the equivalent of Aer Arann, and had an incident-free journey. When we arrived the beauty of the city situated by the Sahara Desert struck me. It was so clean and the air was so different. Fr Mick Waters, who is an SMA priest based, as they say there, about four bush regions out of Kano, met us. Mick was a great hurler and had won an All-Ireland with Cork in 1966, plus several county finals with Blackrock.

The stadium was packed with Nigerians and you could see the odd white face scattered around the place. Some of the Nigerians were very hostile and not at all welcoming. The tension during the match was electric, particularly as we scored first. The Nigerian fans were in a very nasty mood at this stage until the equaliser late into the game. This saved them from embarrassment and perhaps us from execution, as they were getting very ratty towards us. I really feared for our safety if Nigeria were to lose the game. The game went to extra time with no further goals and then on to penalties, which we lost on. A huge party erupted out on the field. We were deflated and exhausted, as we had been sitting for over two hours in the heat, which was over 100°F. We were supposed to have been in the stand but when we arrived we were moved into the middle of the home supporters. Not good for their prospects of hosting the World Cup.

After the game we went to a 'parish hall' where a reception was hosted by a local group. The master of ceremonies was Mick Waters, who proceeded to slag his bishop, an Irish man, who had not gone to the game. The bishop gave an excuse that he didn't want to compromise himself by cheering for one side or the other, but Mick didn't leave him off with that and there was a lot of banter. The team arrived and, though disappointed, soon got into the swing of things and started to unwind. The party continued back at the hotel until the small hours of the morning. I think I went to bed at 4.30 a.m. and had to be up again an hour later for our flight back to Lagos.

We were due to stay in Nigeria for another week but we felt there was no point in staying as all our games were over. When we got back to Lagos we tried to change our tickets and luckily one of the girls in the embassy knew someone in KLM in Lagos and was able to arrange for us to get out that night. We returned to the apartment, which

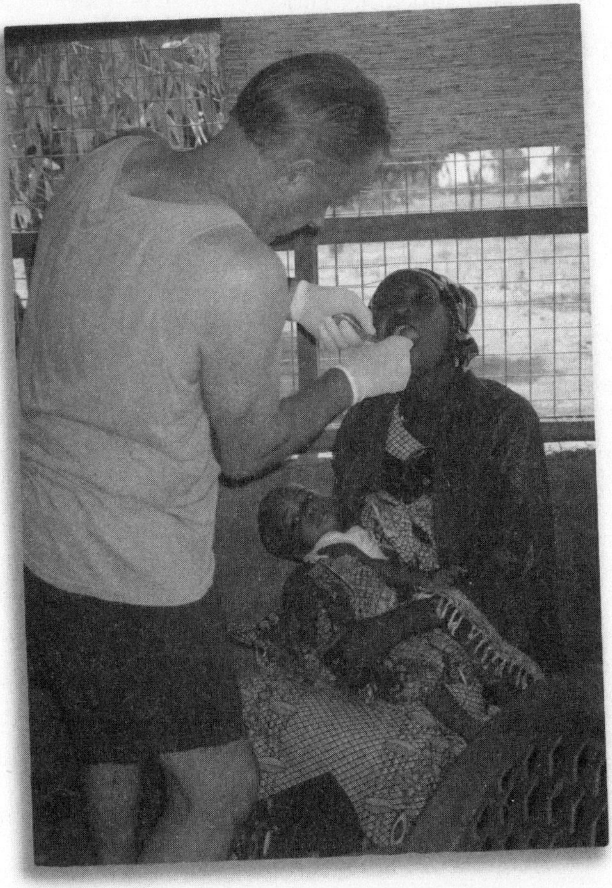

Fr Mick Waters in one of his many roles

we still had two weeks' rent paid on, and packed and waited to be collected and go to the airport. From the city to the airport should take about one hour but it took over three hours. The whole route is a motorway but thousands and thousands of people line the route, selling anything from a pin to a washing machine – anything they could get their hands on. The journey is taken at walking pace. We eventually reached the airport to be met by the Irish team and journalists on their way home too.

When I returned to Cork, I discovered that Cork City were playing against St Pat's in Dublin, so we headed for Inchicore for a match that City should have won. I slept soundly that night.

– 24 –

The Euro 2000 Campaign

After a summer of hurling, football and, of course, work, it was time to start our travels abroad and resume the Euro 2000 campaign, which we did with a 1–0 win in Dublin against Macedonia, followed by a 2–1 win against Yugoslavia.

Our first two matches away were against Croatia and Malta in the one week. We flew first to Malta, where we stayed overnight, and headed back to the airport in Valletta the next morning, and from there flew to Zagreb in Croatia, a beautiful, magnificent city. The match itself was a bit of a disaster as we lost 1–0. At the time I was a selector with the team in Watergrasshill and that night was missing the team playing Youghal in a league final. Who was sitting next to me in Zagreb but Con Spillane who happened to be the manager of the Youghal team. The two of us kept in touch with the game in Cork using Con's mobile phone. We won and I was sorry to have missed the game. We stayed only one night in Zagreb, a city still struggling to come to terms with independence from Yugoslavia and still under threat of invasion by the Serbians.

We arrived back in sunny Malta a few days before the match against the Maltese, so we hired a car and toured the island. Tony, Jerry Mackey and I had an apartment which was close to the beach area. It was noticeable how many English visitors visited Malta, which was once an English colony. We went on a boat trip out to the islands and met some old friends from the midlands, Des Murphy, a retired garda, and his friends. The match itself was a close affair and we were lucky to get out alive, winning 3–2 with a late goal.

The following day we headed home. As we sat in the plane waiting to take off the airport was hit by a severe thunderstorm. The pilot decided to take off in the middle of it and I decided I would keep an eye on one of the air-hostesses as she sat facing me. I thought if she didn't show fear then there was nothing to worry about and this proved to be correct as we got up over the clouds and away from the storm.

That Saturday night I attended a reunion of the Ryan clan in a hotel in Charleville. This had come about at the funeral of my last remaining uncle living in Charleville. We had often spoken about how we only meet at funerals, so one my first cousins, Eamon Fitzpatrick from Newry, took on the responsibility of organising a reunion for all the Ryan first cousins and remaining uncles and aunts.

It turned out to be a truly marvellous night. I would know some of my cousins well, but others live in England and America and we only meet from time to time. Like one morning when I was stationed in Mitchelstown and heading home after night duty. Just at the edge of town these two guys were hitching a lift towards Cork, so I stopped and told them I was going within ten miles of the city.

Some members of the winning Cork team with the Sam Maguire and Liam McCarthy cups in Watercourse Road station in 1990. Back row, from left: Tony O'Sullivan, Tomás Mulcahy, myself, Mick O'Connor, Larry Tompkins, Kieran McGuckian. Front: Shane Kennedy, Brendan, Eoin O'Connor

They sat in. As we got chatting it became clear that they were going to stop off in Watergrasshill to see their uncle who lived there. The nosy person I am, I asked them who might that be as I was from there. 'Jim Ryan,' they said.

The only disappointing aspect of the night for me was I had to leave at about 4 a.m. and head to Cork as I was getting a flight back up to Dublin for the All-Ireland hurling final between Cork and Kilkenny. This was the 1999 final in which Cork, led by an inspirational captain, Mark Landers, took the honours and Mark gave a great speech on accepting the Liam McCarthy cup. After the match I flew back down to Cork and went to work that night, an exhausted but happy man.

Cork also reached the football final that year, only to lose to Meath in a nail-biting game. I think the only match I missed in hurling and football that year was the first round football match against Waterford in Dungarvan. It was a great achievement for the county to get to two finals and be so close to repeating the feat of 1990 in which Cork won the double led by Tomás Mulcahy in hurling and Larry Tompkins in football. I organised a function in the station for Mark and the team – as I had done in 1990 for the double-winning team – and we had a very enjoyable day. Some of the Cork City soccer players joined us as well.

Our last game in the Euro 2000 qualifying group was a match in Skopje, Macedonia. We hadn't been able to get to Skopje in 1997, the last time Ireland played there, and it was looking like it would be difficult again this time. Luckily, a day flight was arranged for the Saturday of the game. We were due to fly out at 7 a.m. and we eventually got away at 9 a.m. – nothing unusual for a charter flight. We took off and the flight seemed to take forever. I felt we were turning and the next thing the pilot announced that we were landing in Rimini, Italy. He later explained that our flight path took us over Yugoslavia and the Serbs had threatened to shoot the plane down if he did not turn back. He didn't have much choice but to land in Rimini to refuel and he then had to get permission to go the long way around.

We landed in Rimini in the fierce heat and were allowed to get off the plane and walk around. We were there for a while and nothing seemed to be happening. The rumour machine started to suggest that we were not getting out of there as the plane was overbooked and the airline would not fly us on as it was too expensive. A sit down was organised as it was felt that if we went into the terminal, the plane would not take off again. We were out on the tarmac for over three hours and eventually the pilot sorted out the problem and off we went, eventually arriving in Skopje Airport about an hour before kick-off. Our tour of the city and our trip down to Kosovo some 20 kilometres from Skopje had to be abandoned. We counted ourselves lucky that we weren't in little pieces, scattered across the Serbian countryside.

We arrived at the grounds about forty minutes before kick-off. I did a quick tour of the stadium as I normally do to pick up programmes and other souvenirs. We were starving but there was very little to eat, so we survived on nuts and beans and something like chicken – not great but it filled a gap. The game was going okay and we led 1–0 up to the last few minutes when we gave away a stupid goal. That put us in the runners-up spot and in to the dreaded play-offs again.

In the play-offs we were drawn against Turkey. The first leg was to be in Dublin followed, four days later, by the second leg in a city called Bursa. The game in Dublin on Saturday, 13 November 1999, ended in a 1–1 draw. On the Monday, Gary, Tony, Brendan and I flew to Budapest with Malav Airlines and onto Istanbul. In the meantime a severe earthquake hit the eastern part of Turkey and the roads became impassable. We got a ferry across from Istanbul to Bsopaus, across the Sea of Marmaru, and from there by bus to Bursa. It was a very long journey but we made the best of it with good craic and conversation, arriving in Bursa to find we were the only Irish in the city.

When we arrived in Bursa we met two Iranians who lived in Germany and who had been following Ireland since Euro '88. They had nowhere to stay so we took them to our hotel and got them a room. We visited some of Bursa's many mosques and had a lovely tour of the city; others opted for a traditional Turkish bath. During our walk around we got a lot of attention as Irish supporters, and met some students who told us of reports in the Irish newspapers that Bursa was not a safe place to visit.

The day before the match we went to the stadium and met a few local officials. I made my way onto the field where there was a group of people gathered in the centre circle. I got in with this crowd who walked with me down to one of the goals and checked it out and then walked up to the other goals and checked it too, then back to the centre circle and back to the stand. I had just done the pre-match inspection with the referee and linesmen and no-one had stopped me! They must have thought I was someone important because the next day as I arrived for the match I was greeted by one of the Turkish officials who welcomed me with open arms and gave me about twenty programmes of the game, which were supposed to be for VIPs only.

The match itself was a dog-eat-dog affair and ended nil-all which meant that Turkey got through on the away goal. This was very disappointing but I think for our sake we were lucky because I don't think the hundred or so of us would have got out alive. The Turks, like the Nigerians in Kano, were vicious and I have no doubt that if we had qualified instead of them that night there would have been severe repercussions for us out there. As it was, they were vicious enough towards us, but we later joined in the celebrations all along the streets of the city.

The return journey the next day was fine until we got on the boat to Istanbul and, just before we docked there, what appeared to be a mini earthquake hit the boat and threw it all over the place. Somehow we took this in our stride and had confidence in the pilot to get us ashore. We eventually docked and got to the airport to find that our plane was delayed by two hours and, as we had only an hour and a half to spare between flights in Budapest, it looked like we would miss our connection. Somehow or another we landed in Budapest with an hour to spare.

It had been another disappointing campaign which put Mick McCarthy as manager under pressure. It's a strange thing about soccer: when the team plays well it gets all the credit, but when it plays badly, it's the manager's fault and he gets sacked. In hurling and football if the players play well they get praised, but if they play badly they get crucified. A lot of this has to do with the press. The GAA press rarely get stuck in a manager, whereas the soccer press are always waiting for the soccer manager to make a mistake.

– 25 –

The Olympic Games

With no Euro 2000 finals to go to, Tony, Jerry and I decided we would head to Australia for the Olympics. It was to be our biggest adventure yet.

We had to forego the first game in the 2002 World Cup campaign against Holland in Amsterdam as we were about to leave for the far side of the world. The players seemed to do all right, even without us, and secured a 2–2 draw.

Our journey began with a flight from Cork to Heathrow, then onto Dubai (what a duty-free!), then to Singapore, landing in Melbourne at 2 a.m. We hung around the airport until morning as we had to pick up a camper van that I had booked from the Skippy Caravan Company. After a sleepless night we picked up the van: a big camper with three double beds, a sitting room area, a kitchen, television set and a toilet and shower. It was an unusual van, Tony's bed was over the cab! We were shown how to service it before we set off to try to find our way out of Melbourne. We got it in one, thanks to Jerry Mackey's ability to read a map. Once we made it to the Hume highway, we pulled into the first service area for something to eat and also decided we would try out the beds in the van. They were so comfortable and we were so tired that we slept for about three hours.

When we woke up we felt better and decided that I would drive for another hour or two as it was about 1,000km to Sydney and would take twelve to fourteen hours non-stop. After a couple of hundred kilometres we pulled into another service station, got some food and decided to stay put. I didn't sleep that well and at about 5 a.m. got up and started to drive. In no time the other two joined me in the cab, defeating my idea of letting them sleep while we got a few miles under us. We stopped for breakfast in a village and shortly after leaving I didn't feel well and had to stop. I had developed a fever so Jerry had to take over the driving. We were told that the closest hospital or doctor was the next town, 120km away.

When we got to the hospital, we were informed that we could go to the A&E to queue for a number of hours or we could go to the out-of-hours doctor up the corridor and pay him and get seen straight away. We took the latter option and he gave me some antibiotics and a prescription and soon I felt fine. He charged me a fair $15. We found a campsite on the outskirts of Sydney and plugged in our camper van to be recharged; this had to be done every few days.

As we needed to get tickets for different events, the next day we headed for a ticket office and queued for five hours. We knew Michael Roche from Cork, Ireland's only boxer in Sydney, was boxing the following day, so that was our first priority. On the day of the fight there was a great Irish crowd in the stadium, which was otherwise nearly empty. Every county jersey and a lot of club jerseys were there. The atmosphere was brilliant but the result went against Michael. We all became 'experts' and blamed the referee.

Our next problem was our van and parking, so after meeting some people from Cork, including Sinead Kidd, the daughter of a friend, John Kidd, we headed to Manley, across the bay from Sydney, where we heard there was a campsite. Manley is a truly beautiful place, much nicer than Bondi Beach, where the only thing of interest was two fellows and a girl hurling – not, it seems, such an unusual sight. At the quayside in Manley there is a saying printed into the wall: 'Manley, seven miles from Sydney, a thousand miles from care.' How true.

Manley became home for us and the camper for the next few weeks. We would park and sleep there overnight and then drive into the outskirts of the town and park the van for the day. There are no clampers in Manley. We discovered that it was easier to get the ferry over to Sydney for $7 a week than to stay there. This was great as each day we went over we saw the competition sailing and one day we got very close to Maria Coleman from Cork, who was lying third at one stage, and had a chat with her. Tickets for the sailing there were $500 each for a day!

One day when we were buying tickets at the ticket desk, based in New Zealand House, we met Helen Clarke who was prime minister of New Zealand. We had a long chat with her and her minister of sport who had a connection with Cork. I presented both of them with 'Hill' ties. This office became our focal point and we seemed to be able to get tickets here for whatever we wanted. We went to some water polo, some soccer and a lot of athletics. The Olympic village was massive and the rail system fantastic.

The highlight had to be the night Sonia O'Sullivan received her medal. There were ten Olympic finals that night and we were lucky enough to get tickets for it. There were 115,000 in the stadium. It started with the pole-vault for women and continued onto Cathy Freeman winning the 400m for women and then Michael Johnson winning the 400m for men. Then came Sonia's race in which she got pipped on the line for gold by Gabriela Szabo.

In my opinion the greatest race of all time was the 10,000m for men where Haile Gebrselassie got up to take it on the line. As Jerry said afterwards, he was led for 9,999 metres. He knew all the time he was going to win and just waited for his moment. I was doing some unpaid work for Neil Prendeville's morning programme on Cork's 96FM and I spoke to him from the stadium before Sonia's race and told him to ring me after the race. I made my way down to the trackside as I saw Sonia was doing a lap of honour. I was willing them to call me, as I knew they were doing the show from Cobh and I was going to get Sonia to say a few words to her mother. A great coup was missed as they didn't telephone me back.

It was tough going though, even for us supporters, as we would be up around six or seven in the morning and

Top: Tony, myself and Jerry in Australia

out for the full day, but we took a few days off here and there. Eating out was a pleasure. One night we went to a restaurant and had a meal of Australian lamb, which is like fillet steak, thick and juicy, nothing like at home.

We went to waterpolo one day but could not get into the rules of it and before we knew it, we had fallen asleep. One of the teams was from Azerbaijan, a place unknown to me at that time but one I would get to know in years to come. We discovered that Manley rugby club was showing the All-Ireland football final between Kerry and Galway at 3 a.m., and the minor final in which Cork were playing, so we parked the van outside the club and went for a nap before the games. Fortunately a phonecall woke us up and we enjoyed both matches.

You never know who you'll bump into in Australia. One day I was on a train sitting next to a woman and we got talking. She asked me about Ireland, which she hoped to visit at some stage. As we chatted I noticed that a few fellows were standing looking at the two of us. I wondered how they knew me, then they approached us and asked this lady for her autograph. She was Shane Gould, the Australian swimmer who had won five gold medals in a previous Olympics!

As tickets for the closing ceremony were selling at around $700 we decided we would give it a skip and instead headed up Blue Mountain to finish off our tour of Sydney. We gave climbing Sydney Bridge a miss as we thought it was too expensive, and we drove up the mountain for about two hours wondering what we were supposed to look for. We stopped when we spotted a McDonalds and decided we had driven long enough and headed back down and onto the Princess Highway, the coast road between Sydney and Melbourne. That evening we stopped in a village to watch the closing ceremony of the Olympics in a pub with a few others.

Next day we drove on and headed for Cowes on Philip Island. Here we were to witness the most amazing natural spectacle called the Penguin Parade. Each morning at dawn the penguins head out to sea for the day and arrive home at dusk. Just as it was getting dark we sat near the strand watching each wave breaking gently. Suddenly a wave came in, broke and started to ebb back out to reveal hundreds of beautiful penguins. If one of the group does not arrive, the rest wait for him to arrive on the next wave and then they all make their way home. When they are all in, people walk across specially designed walkways and you can see the penguins close up. It was a fabulous experience. We took the van back to the depot and headed to Melbourne Airport after a very enjoyable trip down under.

On the way home, we stopped in Dubai and, as I had not slept on the flight, I wanted to wash. I did so in the most unlikely place. Muslims don't usually use toilet paper, believing it to be unhygienic, and instead use a hand-held water spray similar to what we use for washing hair. I went into the toilet in Dubai Airport, saw this thing in a cubicle, and not knowing at the time what it was, took out my passport and money out of my shirt and put them on top of a ledge. I took off my shirt and got down on my knees and proceeded to wash my hair into the toilet. I felt great after this shower. After drying my hair I walked along the airport to discover that I had left my passport and money in the loo. Panic set in and I ran back. The cubicle was occupied, but to my relief my passport and money were still there.

You can buy anything in Dubai Airport. It even has an Irish bar. Jerry Mackey paid a visit there and found that no-one spoke Irish or English. As we were disembarking in Dubai, I noticed a lot of women and children in a special area in the departures lounge who later got on our flight. They did not look very happy. When the plane was in the air I went back to them and tried to talk to them but they refused to say anything and all got off in Singapore. I never found out what was making them so unhappy.

We arrived in London, shattered, but Tony and I decided to go to Lisbon for the Ireland v Portugal match. Jerry wanted to see the Cork county hurling final which was on the Sunday, so we let him off. As it happened, that game was postponed for a week so I got to see it in any case. Meanwhile, Tony and I were joined in London by Mairead O'Callaghan and we headed off to Lisbon. As I had not slept for over two days I was totally disorientated and wondered where we were when we landed.

We found our hotel, got a new lease of life and headed out for a while, but soon the tiredness caught up with us. The replay of the All-Ireland final which we had seen in Manley was on the Saturday and some enterprising Irishman had decided he would set up a big screen and get us all to watch it. We found where the showing was, in a big square near the docklands, but they were charging £20 to go inside the barriers. We said ‘no thanks’ and watched the game from outside the barriers for free. It wasn’t going to cost us that much to go into the soccer game that night!

The match turned out to be a great game in which we came back to score a great equaliser and continue our run towards the World Cup of 2002. On the Sunday we came back to Heathrow, got our bags from storage and put them on the flight to Cork. Unfortunately the bags went to Dublin. All the way from Australia and the bags get lost on the shortest leg of the journey!

– 26 –

The Road to Japan

As the start of 2000 was a quiet one on the international front, with only a number of friendlies, Tony and I headed to Brest in France to cheer on Brian Kerr's under-18 team which included John O'Shea, Andy Reid and Liam Miller. On this trip we were accompanied by Tony's niece and nephew, Yvonne and Eric McNulty.

We took my car and headed off on the ferry to Brest. We had a job finding the team hotel which was about twenty miles away, very isolated and not at all in the glamorous surroundings a professional footballer might hope for. As in Nigeria, we were the only supporters apart from parents and friends of the players; a fact acknowledged by Brian Kerr in his programme notes for the return leg in Dublin. The match itself was a great game and ended up nil-all, giving us high expectations for the return match in Tolka Park the following week. But it wasn't to be as France put away an early goal and our planned trip to Argentina the following year for the World Cup finals was put away with it.

After two draws away to Holland and Portugal, our

first World Cup qualifier home game was against Estonia in Dublin, which we won 2–0. In March 2001 we had a two-game trip to Cyprus and Andorra. We flew to Heathrow and then onto Cyprus, where we hired a car and did a tour of the country. We found a village up a mountain where we met a man who was the local vet, doctor, carpenter, mechanic, just about anything you wanted, and he was also the supplier of the local mountain brew, which he got for us. We also went to visit Northern Cyprus but were not allowed cross over as, after midday, we were too late. We eventually got across when we returned to Cyprus in 2005.

As we were driving into Nicosia we passed the stadium and decided to visit. It was a beautiful stadium with a double roof, which covers 10,000 seats, and a running track next to it. I made my way up to the top of the stadium and into the press room where I lifted the phone and got a line. I made a few quick calls to people at home, who were not impressed with me as I had forgotten the time difference – it was early on a Saturday morning. We later returned to the stadium for the game, which was a bit one-sided and Ireland ran out easy winners 4–0.

The days after the game we enjoyed the sunshine of Cyprus and then headed back to London to get our connecting flight to Barcelona where the Andorra match was to be played (there was no stadium big enough in Andorra). We arrived in Barcelona Airport on the Wednesday of the match, hired a car and found Neu Camp in one go. The match itself was like a home game with so many

Irish supporters and a great atmosphere. The Andorra side had no support and we ran out easy winners 3–0.

After the match we got out of the city and found somewhere to stay in a village on the coast about forty miles from Barcelona. We made this home for a few days until it was time to leave Barcelona and all its sights and return to Cork.

The month after this trip we played the return leg with Andorra in Dublin and beat them 3–1. Then, in June 2001, we had double engagement, playing and drawing with Portugal 1–1 in Dublin and then heading off to Tallinn in Estonia for the return leg against them. Tallinn is a most beautiful place; the city is divided into two with an old city and a new. The old city is really nice and has the old Russian feel to it. We stayed in a hotel situated in a forest a few miles from the city – a beautiful setting.

Tallinn is across the Gulf of Finland from Helsinki and you could go there on a day trip by ferry, but we decided against it as we wanted to see more of Tallinn's museums and churches. The match was played in what appeared to be a building site: a new, unfinished stadium. There was a doubt that the match would even be played. We were destroyed with dust but managed to win 2–0.

Our next match was against Holland in Dublin on 1 September. It was a very tense game and we needed a good result to stay in the tournament. We got it when Jason McAteer scored a great goal to stun the Dutch. The barricades went up in defence and we ran out winners.

Our last game in the group was a home game against

Cyprus, which we won 4–0 to put us in the dreaded play-offs again. This time it was to be a whole new experience as we were drawn against Iran in a two-legged play-off. The first game was to be played in Dublin on 10 November 2001 and the second in Tehran the following Wednesday.

Myself, Jerry and Tony in Barcelona

Gary Spain and I decided we would go, despite the fact that some of the travel agents had told everyone it would not be safe and that the Irish would be in big danger. Cobblers! After the first game in Dublin, which Ireland won 2–0, we headed off on the Monday to Frankfurt in Germany to get our flight to Tehran. In Frankfurt we met a few other 'brave' Paddies who hadn't listened to the advice of the travel agents. We knew that people flew in and out of Tehran every day of the week and survived, although there was one brief moment of hesitation as we walked down the terminal and saw on the television screen that another plane had crashed in New York. I said to Gary that we were safe now as it was unlikely that two planes would crash on the same day. That was just a short time after 9/11, so people were still scared about flying.

We had a pleasant flight to Tehran and it was noticeable that about half an hour before landing there was a big rush by the women on board to cover up and put their headgear on. Up to this it was like any other flight. When we got off the flight there was no problem going through customs or police checks. Gary had organised an apartment through a friend of his who had arranged for the landlord to pick us up. True to his word, Robert was waiting for us at the terminal in his Manchester United jersey.

Alcohol is not allowed in Iran, but the amount that was consumed on our six-hour flight was amazing, as was the fact that when we arrived at our apartment there were bottles of wine, liquor and some gin in the cabinet – all in a country where alcohol is outlawed. This was even more amusing as I don't drink and Gary rarely does.

Next morning after a lie in and a good breakfast, we ventured out onto the streets. We were told by the Department of Foreign Affairs that the only danger in Tehran was in crossing the road. How true this was. Did you ever wonder where all the Hillman-Hunters cars that were in Ireland in the 1970s disappeared to? They appear to have turned up in Tehran. The traffic is horrendous but we soon got the knack of crossing the road. Cars drive everywhere: three lanes of traffic on a street can easily turn into six lanes as they all vie for position; it was fascinating to watch.

We were welcomed with open arms by the Iranians and they were very hospitable. Gary and I were inside a shop once when we met a woman and her two teenage daughters. We had good banter with them and as we were leaving we shook hands with the two daughters, but the mother refused so I teased her about it. It was something to do with the Islamic religion. Eventually I turned away and offered my hand to her and she took it.

Our host, Robert, took us to an Indian restaurant where we had a full meal which cost about $17 for the three of us. Robert's wife never wears headgear in the house, but once she goes outside, it's put on. Robert took us on a tour of the city and showed us the British embassy, which used to be on Winston Churchill Street, but in the 1980s, much to the astonishment of the British government, the name of the street was changed to Bobby Sands Street. Apparently the Iranians hold Bobby Sands in very high esteem and were surprised when we told them he wasn't a national hero in Ireland.

On the day of the match an RTÉ camera crew arrived at our apartment to film Gary and me during our stay in Tehran; they wanted to see Irish supporters in a domestic setting in downtown Tehran. They filmed us in the apartment and I showed them around, including in the toilet which was a hole in the ground. It would be hard to perform there if you had a cruciate ligament problem! Then we went onto a sports shop to pick up some Iranian jerseys. We had great craic there and there was enough chat to sustain the whole programme. We had no Farsi and they had no English but we communicated very well for about an hour. We were then taken to a newspaper office where the chief sports editor was a woman. Women are not allowed into sporting events so she had to watch it on television instead, reporting on it from the screen. We were then brought to an Iranian restaurant where we sampled Larry Goodman's beef steak and potatoes. The film crew met us afterwards at the match and their work was shown sometime later on RTÉ. It was called *Big in Tehran* – I wondered if it was Gary and my size that helped to name the programme.

We decided to get a taxi to the Azadi Stadium, arrived quite early and kept our taxi man for our return journey. He must have been one of the few Iranians who had no interest in the match. We were amongst the first Irish into the stadium and at this stage, about two and a half hours before kick-off, the stadium was three-quarters full. A lot of the Iranians had been there since the night before and had camped outside the grounds.

As we were the first away fans to visit the Azadi in many years, we were applauded early on. However later, as we approached them to shake hands, some of the locals turned hostile and started firing apples and oranges at us. We were up in the gods on the halfway line but it must have been hard for the players to see or hear us.

Then an ice-breaking moment in world football came when our eight Irish women entered the ground and got a good reception, not alone from us, but from the Iranian supporters who were near us. Another Irish woman made history down on the field when Donna McBride, an Irish freelance photographer, became the first female journalist allowed into a sports event in Iran. The atmosphere was both electric and intimidating as the teams took the field, but it was nothing compared to when the whole stadium recited a prayer from the Koran. If ever you want the hairs to stand on the back of your head, get in the middle of 80,000 Iranians reciting the Koran. You will never experience anything like it.

A banner saying '3–0' was unfolded behind one of the goals; this was what the Iranians believed would be the scoreline and they had come prepared. The Irish supporters numbered about 500, including celebrities like Eddie Jordan and Denis O'Brien. It was here that I first met Damien the Doc, who was to become a great friend and travelling companion. The game itself was very tense, the hopeful 3–0 scoreline appeared on the big electric scoreboard, but it wasn't to be: the Iranians got a consolation goal late on and then attacked again but to no avail. We held out and won 2–1 on aggregate. At long last, after all the play-offs, we had reached another finals, again to be held in Japan and Korea.

Early on in the match I had put my eye on a big banner in Farsi and English which said 'Islamic Republic of Iran – Irish Fans Section' and as soon as the game was over, I went over and took it. It is now one of my prized possessions. We located our very tired and bored taxi driver who dropped us at our apartment. He only wanted $8 for the day, so when we gave him $25 his eyes lit up and he got a new lease of life. On the way to our apartment about ten miles of the highway was covered in glass – apparently as a protest against the government. It is commonplace for windscreens to be broken for this reason.

The next morning Gary and I were up at 4 a.m. for a trip to Esfahan. The journey cost us $50, including an hour's flight and a guide for the day. An Irish travel agent had told us he would do the same trip for $200 – quite a difference. Before I went to Iran I had an operation for an ingrown toenail and infection, and while in Iran it flared up. I had to go to the community-based hospital where I got the best of attention and was charged the lordly sum of $1. When we were on the way to the airport for our flights to Esfahan, the taxi driver refused to take money from us as he said it was an honour to have the Irish in his car and we were very welcome. However, we forced him to take the money. Some day I hope I meet a taxi man in Ireland who will be so honoured to have me in his car that he will not charge me.

When we arrived in Esfahan, after a lovely flight with Iran Air, our guide was waiting for us and off we went on a tour of one of the most beautiful cities in the world. Esfahan was the capital of the old Persian empire and it is thought to be in the middle of the world. It has the second biggest square in the world after Tianneman Square, with many palaces, minarets and mosques dating from the early centuries, each with its century's own distinctive design. We finished our exhausting day with a visit to a teahouse on the dried-up River Zagandeh. There were a lot of different types of tea, which looked suspiciously like something else. I had never had tea through a tube which came out like smoke, so I went for the bottled water instead.

We left with nothing but brilliant memories of a wonderful few days in Iran.

– 27 –

2002 World Cup, Japan

Cameroon, Germany and Saudi Arabia were drawn to make up our group in Japan so I was not too confident of our prospects. Still, a supporter is a supporter and I was going to support the boys in green to the end. I knew the team was going on holiday before going to the finals, so I was surprised when the whole Saipan affair took place. It was amazing that everyone, even people who had not the slightest idea about football, had an opinion about what happened out there and still have serious debates on the subject. For me, the manager is the boss and players should respect him, even when they think he is wrong. In this case, I think Roy Keane was wrong.

Tony O'Sullivan, Jerry Mackey and I travelled to Japan via Dublin and Frankfurt, arriving in Norita Airport outside Tokyo. Like us, Vince Cummins, Tony Fitzgerald, Eddie McGough and Mick Hanley were going to hire a car at the airport so we planned to go in convoy. It was with trepidation that we left the airport but I had complete faith in Jerry Mackey's ability to read maps, even if they were in Japanese. We found the road we needed and drove on very slowly as the amount of traffic on this untolled road was unbelievable. It's a well known fact that there are far more cars than space in Japan. We drove for a couple of hours and found a hotel for the night.

The next day the two cars headed for Niigata, with Irish flags up on the car so we could see each another. We were told before we went out that FIFA had pre-booked hotel rooms all over Japan and accommodation would be hard to find. We finally got rooms in what was called a Love Hotel which are used by Japanese couples who want a bit of privacy away from their crammed apartments. You can hire these rooms for as little as one or two hours, so imagine the surprise on the hotel owner's face when seven big Irish men arrived to share two rooms with all mod cons for an intimate evening! The heat in the rooms was intense and I found it hard to sleep so I took a walk around Niigata in the middle of the night. I came back to the car and tried to sleep in that but to no avail. It must have been the thought of being stuck in a Love Hotel with six big men but we got a great laugh over the fact that we stayed in one of those hotels and were not afraid to admit to having stayed there.

The Japanese had a great transport system for the games. Everyone got buses to the grounds, with no delay. There was great colour and excitement at the Cameroon match and in a swelter of excitement it ended 1–1. After the match we left Niigata and headed down the motorway, through a fifteen kilometre long tunnel and through the worst hailstorm I had ever seen. We got through it and found a beautiful five-star hotel in a closed ski resort by chance and stayed there that night for around €30 each.

I had booked an apartment in Yohohama for the duration of our stay there, beginning the next day. We had an address on the outskirts of Tokyo and I asked a number of drivers for directions. One of them, a man and his daughter, said he would show us. With the daughter waving out through the roof window, we followed them in and out of traffic for nearly an hour until we landed outside the apartment. What a kind gesture, but they took off before we could properly thank them.

We had a three-bedroomed apartment with no beds, just the floor to sleep on. The house rules included no shoes in the apartment and keeping it clean. One evening we had a wine and cheese reception in the apartment and the place was so clean we had it sitting on the floor. There were a number of other Paddies staying in the apartments and our main trouble was expensive parking. We got around it by putting it into the park by night and leaving it at the side of the street by day – illegal, but with Irish flags we got away with it. I learned that you have a half hour grace after they mark the spot where the car is parked, so all you had to do was move it a little. In Japan, bicycles are one of the main modes of transport so they have bicycle wardens too – if you leave your bike too long it will get a ticket.

The first night we were walking up the street and found a lovely little bar which would seat six with six standing. The owner, Luigi from Korea, later told me that he would normally sell one and a half barrels of beer a week, but by the time all the Paddies had called on their way in and out of the city, he was selling ten barrels a night. He did a great trade and showed his appreciation by producing food for the lads, taking us on walking tours and driving tours of Japan and being generally most helpful. He even closed the pub for a day to take us on one long tour. He showed me how to get to Ibaraki stadium, out in the wilds, which we had passed the first day we arrived. I forgot to ask him how long it would take so we left at 11 a.m. for the match against Germany at 8.30 p.m., thinking it would take about five hours. I arrived there at 12.30, a full eight hours before the game, but it worked out well as there was entertainment laid on such as Irish, German and Japanese entertainers, including Geisha Girls in their traditional costume. The security to get into the match was ridiculous and it took ages. There were only 32,000 supporters, but it took us about two hours to get into the grounds.

However, inside the grounds there was a great atmosphere, with thousands of Irish supporters. Germany scored early and as the match neared the end it looked as thought defeat was going to be our lot. Then up comes Robbie Keane to score a great goal, stunning the Germans and sending the Paddies into great celebration and announcing our arrival on the world stage of soccer. It was a very happy two carloads of Irish who left Ibaraki and headed back towards Yokohama.

We called to our little pub for a celebration drink and went back to the apartment to the very comfortable beds on the floor – no harm that night as at least we couldn't fall out of them. I had some of the best nights' sleep on these floors that I ever had.

The final match in our group was against Saudi Arabia in Yokohama. We got the train out to the stadium and met Damien the Doc, and Gary and Tara Spain who had produced a programme for the World Cup which they were selling as we went in. The official programmes were €20 each and jerseys were selling at €90, so the full experience was a bit pricey.

Once again there was a huge crowd of Irish supporters in the stadium, and great atmosphere. I did a live link-up from the stadium with Neil Prendeville on 96FM and I was only barely able to hear him over all the noise. The match itself was an easy victory for us, 3–0, and will be remembered by all for the gesture made by Damien Duff to the Japanese fans after he had scored a goal, when he went behind the goals, put his hands together and bowed his head Japanese style. What a compliment to pay to our hosts who, even without that, will always remember the Irish team and its supporters.

Before I went out to Japan I knew that if we qualified out of our group we would be playing in Korea, so I had booked us all to fly to Seoul the day after the Saudi game. Even if we didn't qualify I reckoned we would have a few days holiday in Korea. On arrival in Seoul airport, we had nowhere to stay, but a very helpful lady in the information centre in the airport got us a hotel in the city centre for the duration of our stay.

We arrived at the hotel to discover that it was part of

Some pics from Korea

a Buddhist monastery, beautiful and clean, again without beds. The Buddhist temple was done up in great colour for the World Cup and each night they had a big screen on the open-air altar to show a match. When Korea was playing, the head Buddha would honour us with his presence.

Seoul is the fifth biggest capital city in the world with a population of ten and a half million, yet there is little or no crime; one day we watched as ten policemen arrived on their Honda 50s to deal with one drunk. There was great excitement anytime that Korea was playing and big screens were placed all around the city so people could watch the games. Millions of people came out to watch. There was no alcohol allowed and no-one drank. On the night Korea beat Italy, we watched the game in the temple and it was a great thrill to be there but nothing compared to the celebration on the street afterwards where over two million Koreans were celebrating. When they saw us in our green jerseys, they came over and shook our hands which were mighty sore the next day.

We went for something to eat that night but when my chicken arrived it looked suspiciously like dog, as I have never seen a chicken with a leg that big. Tony Fitzgerald reckoned it was definitely dog as next day he was able to run quickly instead of walk slowly. We also paid a visit to the North Korea border, which was a great experience. It was in this area that the programme *MASH* was based.

In the draw for the 1/16 round we were drawn against Spain in a place called Suwon about thirty miles from Seoul. We headed off by train, which cost €1 return. Again

Back row: Damien Green, Gary Spain and myself in Tehran with other fans

the place was jointed with Irish, as more had arrived over here from home and it was like a home match. There was a great party atmosphere and as word came from home that it was lashing rain, it made it even more pleasurable to be in 70°F heat. The match itself was tense as it ended 1–1, then went to extra time with no golden or silver goal scored. Then came the most horrible of ways to decide a match, penalties, which of course we lost. Our dream of being World Cup champions came to an end and we headed home to Ireland after a very exciting and hospitable time in Asia.

– 28 –

Oslo, 2004

Before Japan, I had been at a European under-19 qualifier in Cork. Ireland, under the management of Brian Kerr and Noel O'Reilly, were in group fourteen with Austria, Croatia and Latvia. They won those three matches and then had to face Holland in an intermediary round home and away. In the first match in Rotherham players such as Stephen Kelly (Spurs), Stephen Paisley (Man. City), Sean Thornton (Sunderland), Liam Kearney (Nott's Forest), and Stephen Elliott, put on a great display and beat the Dutch 2–1. So we were all set up for the return match in Cork. A huge crowd gathered in Turner's Cross for a very tense game. It ended nil-all and Ireland qualified for the European Under-19 Championships to be held in Norway.

And so the three of us headed off to Oslo. We thought Japan had been expensive but it was nothing compared to the prices in Norway. A car in Japan had cost us €400 for the duration, whereas the renting of a car in Norway cost over €600 for one week. Main course meals were €30 and a stamp was €1.30.

We picked up the car in Oslo Airport and headed to

Drammen, which is an hour's drive from Oslo, as were all the venues for the games. We found the only hotel in this lovely city and after staying the first night at a huge price we struck a good deal for the whole stay which worked out at about €50 per night.

Our first match against Belgium ended in a nil-all draw, and then it was onto a town called Moss to take on the star-studded Germans in what turned out to be a disappointing loss. After this we headed to Hanefoss for the game against England who got off to a great start with two goals. However, they didn't realise how stubborn the Irish were, especially a small fellow from Cork called Kearney who dazzled the Brits with his skill. We scored three second-half goals to stun the English and qualify for the bronze medal position against Slovakia on the Sunday, which we unfortunately lost.

During our week stay, we went on a number of trips, including one with the team at the invitation of Brian and Noel. We went to the site of the winter Olympics and climbed all the way up to the top of the competition ski slope. What a view there was, and what a nerve you would need to stand up there and start skiing right down the mountain. We also went on a boat trip on the Fjords and saw the dramatic high rock formations hanging over the clear blue water, with quaint wooden houses built on the coastline.

Unlike other international teams, there is always a party attitude in all Irish camps as soon as the serious work of playing is done. This under-19 trip was no exception and each night, once the players were tucked up in bed, there would be a sing-song in the lobby. It was fascinating to watch the reaction of the other countries' delegations as they looked on at how we Irish enjoyed ourselves. On our last night the players were given their freedom to go out on the town. It was funny to see the whole panel go out for the night, and return after half an hour, exhausted and bored. Meanwhile Noel O'Reilly produced the guitar and a sing-song began. We were joined by some of the other delegations, particularly when Willie Kearney, Liam's father, produced his button accordion and started playing. A great night and week with a fourth place finish.

– 29 –

European Championships

When we got back it was time to book for the European Championships and so, in early September, we found ourselves on a plane to Moscow for Ireland's first match.

We were warned to be careful when we got to Moscow Airport as there are a lot of chancers who offer to take you anywhere you want to go but at a huge price. We found a nice man who had a genuine taxi and he took us to our hotel, which was three quarters of an hour away, for $50 between the five of us which was good value. The hotel was basic, but it did us fine – no ensuite here, every two rooms had to share a bathroom. The hotel was across the road from the metro station, and the trains ran every few minutes. It cost the equivalent of thirteen cent to get to Red Square, about twenty minutes away.

Moscow is a dangerous city, and some of the Irish were robbed or conned. I met one couple who had handed over their Visa card to a taximan for payment and it was a day before they realised that he had taken a couple of thousand euros out of their account. We visited Lenin's tomb and the grave of an unknown soldier, continuing our practice of

Above: Moscow; Below: Changing of the guard in Red Square

paying our respects to other soldiers' graves in places we visit like Paris, Brussels and Taillin. There is a great tradition in Moscow that when couples get married they go to Red Square for photographs. One day we witnessed about fifty wedding parties all trying to take photographs at the changing of the guard, which is a great spectacle.

On our first night we called to a pub near our hotel and had a great night with ten of the locals. While we were working on East/West relations, Damien the Doc was negotiating elsewhere in Moscow to get us invited to a reception in the Irish embassy. He succeeded and we turned up at this official reception in our Irish jerseys and shorts. We were probably the only genuine supporters present; most of the others were dolled up to the nines. The ambassador, Jim Sharkey, made us feel at home and welcomed us warmly. Also present were a few VIPs such as Michael Flatley, Lisa Murphy and Paul Brady.

We also met a fascinating man from west Cork who had come to Russia some years previously and bought five acres about four hours outside of Moscow. When we met him he had access to 60,000 acres and was quite happy living and farming there. On the train the next day we met a man who told us his name was Marcus. He was a priest working about 800km from Moscow, and had been chaplin in Cork University Hospital the year before!

The Russians are full of bureaucracy and when we arrived at the ground for the match a full hour and a half before kick-off, they insisted on checking each Irish supporter with an x-ray machine, which didn't work a lot of the time, with the result that most of us missed the start of the game.

The game was a disaster as we were beaten, destroyed, 4–2 by the Russians. To add insult to injury, they insisted on keeping all the Irish inside the stadium after the match, like sheep in a pen, which was not well received. They started to play music over the public address system, starting with the Manfred Mann's 'There she was walking down the street' and the whole atmosphere changed. The Irish party started and at the end we did not want to leave – it was one of the best outdoor discos ever! There had never been a problem with the Irish fans and we are lucky that we have an easy temperament and accept whatever happens.

Moscow is a great place, particularly Red Square, for people selling caps and badges of clubs and countries. While having a cuppa in an outdoor café in Red Square, this guy came up to me and offered to sell me badges. I had a look and in the middle of his collection was a Cork City/Dynamo Kiev badge from the time Cork City played out there. I bought it from him and added it to my collection.

Our next match in this group was against Switzerland in Dublin which was a bad game for us and we ended up losing 2–1. In soccer when the players win, they get all the praise but when the players play badly the manager is sacked and so Mick McCarthy followed the footsteps of John Giles and Eoin Hand. The quest to find his successor began.

A whole lot of different names were mentioned, including Bobby Robson and Kevin Moran, but my personal favourite for the job was Brian Kerr. I thought it was a natural progression from the youths and under-age teams

Scenes from Moscow

to the senior job. He had also worked with a lot of these players when they were starting off. I was delighted when he was announced as the new manager and everyone seemed happy he had got the job, including the FAI, media, players and fans. His first match in charge was an away game against Scotland, which had been arranged before he got the job. Word had it that Brian had talked to Roy Keane with a view to getting him up to Scotland to meet the new management team and players and try to sort out their differences.

On the eve of the game there was an under-21 match in Kilmarnock which Tony, Gary and I went to. We stayed with my nephew and godson, Barry Murphy, who at this stage was working in Glasgow. Like his brother, Donal, Barry had won All-Ireland medals with Cork minors and under-21s. Just as Tony, Gary and I were going into the under-21 game we had a word with Brian Kerr and wished him well and he thanked us for our support, as he always did. I then got a phonecall from a reporter I knew and he asked me for a comment regarding the statement which had just been released by Roy Keane saying he had changed his mind about playing for Ireland.

Brian's career got off to the best possible start with the game in Glasgow, when the team won 2–0. This was to be the start of his all too short reign as manager of the Irish team. Tony and I stayed in Scotland for a few more days and took in the Triple Crown match in Edinburgh between Scotland and Ireland. Ireland hammered the Scots in that game but picked up the wooden spoon in the championship.

– 30 –

Camogie and Hockey

It was only in the 1960s that the first camogie club was formed in Watergrasshill. A number of women from the area were playing with other clubs so it seemed a logical step. At that stage in camogie they used to wear those horrible pinafores and black tights. The Hill girls had brown skirts, yellow tops and black tights – a slight improvement on the pinafore. They had a few good players and in no time they had been crowned County Junior Champions. The disappointment came when all they got was nothing bigger than an eggcup. A bigger cup had to be found for the customary parade through the village.

The girls progressed well through the years rising to intermediate and then to senior, but the County Senior Championship eluded them. As the older girls retired and the younger ones started playing, they also took up ladies football and in the late 1970s won the County Junior title and the next year played in the senior grade. This was the year when they got to both county semi-finals. As there was a conflict between the camogie board and the ladies football board, both games were fixed for the same day at different venues miles apart. So, having played the camogie match in the morning, all the girls drove to the next venue to play in the football series. These girls were dedicated and fit and some of them went on to play with Cork in both games and win All-Ireland medals. In 1980/81 they won the County Senior Football final and we had a great year following them up and down the country. They progressed to the All-Ireland Senior Club final where they played and beat Galway Gaels. It was a great achievement for a very dedicated bunch of girls.

My four nieces, Fiona, Eimear, Sinead and Áine Connery, were also very good camogie players but it was in hockey that they really excelled. Their mother, my sister Kathleen, had been a great athlete and in her younger days even took on and beat the boys at the local athletic events.

In 2003, Fiona made the Irish senior hockey team for the European finals in Barcelona, so Tony and I headed off to support the girls in green, along with my two sisters, Kathleen and Mary. After all the years following Irish teams it was great to see one of your own playing for Ireland. It's a pity the national anthem is not played at these games. Instead, as at rugby matches, they play this stupid 'Ireland's Call' which I refuse to stand for as it is not a national anthem but a poor substitute. It's ironic that when we play England in rugby or hockey we all stand to attention for 'God Save the Queen', but we have nothing to stand for for our own team. It was really great to see Fiona in the green for Ireland and I have seen her many times since. It took me a while to get into the rules of hockey but I am getting there.

Fiona and Áine's club was Hermes in Dublin and when they qualified for the European Cup in Baku in Azerbaijan, Tony and I headed to Prague to meet up with the team and take them on a tour of the city. I had visited Prague about three weeks beforehand so I knew my way around. We visited the castle for the changing of the guard at midday, which is spectacular, and then went to the Infant of Prague Church, then back over Charles Bridge to see the Astronomical Clock in the old square.

Our flight to Baku was later that night, arriving in Baku at 5 a.m. As in most of these countries there is always a charge to enter the country which in this case was $20. Tony and I were taken to our hotel, which was the old communist headquarters in the main square looking out at the Caspian Sea. Also staying in our hotel were members of the Uzbekistan soccer teams who were playing Azerbaijan the following day. The city is in an oil-rich country, but the water was very oily and dirty too. If they managed to clean the sea, the country could really take off, tourist-wise, like other former Soviet states such as Estonia, Lithuania and Latvia.

Ladas were the most popular car in Baku and all the buildings were grey. In one of these we found an Irish pub but no-one spoke Irish or English so we found a lovely English pub and had a beautiful meal. We searched Baku for an Azerbaijan jersey but to no avail; we could find one from any club in Europe but not the national one.

The city has its quirks. One day while on our way to the hockey stadium, I saw a policeman stopping a car at a checkpoint. The driver got out of the car, walked up to the policeman and gave him a kiss on the cheek. The policeman then proceeded to give the driver a ticket. It never happened to me!

Hermes were beaten in the final, so later Tony and I decided to go to the soccer match in the stadium. It was nearly half time and there were still thousands outside waiting to get in once the gates opened to let them in for free. We had bought our match tickets earlier for the princely sum of fifty cents each. However, the average monthly wage there is about $60, so matches were a luxury.

I approached two police officers and in my good Irish jersey and broken English tried to explain that we were VIPs and needed to get in. With that a clearway was forced open and we were soon inside the grounds. I eyeballed a steward inside the VIP box and made hand gestures to him which are universal when you are trying to get somewhere you shouldn't be. He understood my gestures and we landed inside the special area, where we picked up programmes and team sheets. Though this was only a friendly, there was a big crowd including what seemed to be the whole government cabinet and the Sultan.

We found a position in front of the cabinet ministers and got talking to them. When they saw our Irish jerseys they were very interested as Azerbaijan was drawn to play Northern Ireland and the conversation centred around the North and South.

One of the ministers was drinking a pale liquid and I asked what it was. He said it was tea and offered me some.

I had tried this tea already and it was not nice, more like washing-up liquid, but when a minister of a country asks you to have some tea, it's polite to accept. His waiter arrived back with tea and biscuits, which we had to swallow.

It was a great match and Azerbaijan won out 3–1. After the match we were the centre of attention with our Irish flag and jerseys. Everyone seemed to want to take photographs of the two of us, including about a hundred policemen, who stood into the photo. While this was going on I spotted the Uzbekistan team bus leaving, so I stopped it and asked for a lift back to the hotel. It was an old banger which just about got us back safely but we were very grateful. I also managed to pick up a few souvenirs from them.

The night before the final hockey match there was a state banquet to which Tony and I were invited, along with the teams. We were picked up at our hotel by the bus carrying the Hermes team, who had adopted us as their uncles. We headed off and drove through the slums on the outskirts of the city, where we saw people sleeping in tents with open sewers nearby. In the middle of all this was a magnificent stately home. We went in with all our nieces and were greeted by the best musicians, singers and dancers in the land. I counted thirty-two courses to eat and Tony and I made a good attempt at the lot of them.

After the formalities and banquet, there was dancing and all the teams were enjoying themselves except the Russian team who were very reserved. A few of them went out dancing so I went out and joined them, got an Irish flag, and gave it to one of them. I got them to bring out the Russian flag and Fiona and a few of the girls joined in. Soon all the teams had their national flags out on the floor and each team took another country's flag. Once the ice was broken everyone had a great night.

We arrived back in Prague and tried to do a tour but instead headed to the airport and fell asleep having eaten a great breakfast in Murphy's Irish pub near the Infant of Prague church, cooked by a young man from Crosshaven.

– 31 –

THE HEINEKEN CUP

In 2003, a new airline started up in Cork called JetMagic. I heard they were to auction their inaugural flights on their new jets to fly people to Toulouse in France for the Heineken Cup Series semi-final, Munster v Toulouse. I was not a huge rugby fan but I had become interested through watching Munster playing on television, though I still think that they play what I call a very gaelic type of rugby. In other words they play with passion and they play like a club gaelic football or hurling team, and like playing for the honour of their provinces.

I went on the internet and found the JetMagic website where I put in a bid for three tickets and was successful. All the money raised was to go to Marymount Hospice in Cork, my favourite charity, as my mother and father had both died there and my brother Mick was chaplain there at one stage.

And so it was that on Saturday, 26 April 2003, I headed to Cork Airport with Brendan and Mairead O'Callaghan who took the other seats from me. We were wined and dined early in the morning, with a Champagne reception beforehand and a fanfare to our state-of-the- art thirty-nine-seater jet. We were treated like royalty on the first flight ever for this company. I was even taken up to the cockpit and shown around and it was fascinating to see how a plane stays in the air. I could see a plane right in front of us but the pilot explained it was actually twenty miles ahead and that there was another one twenty miles behind. I was like a child in total wonderment of it all.

On arrival in Toulouse we were collected by bus from the plane and taken to the stadium, where we enjoyed even more hospitality before the match. In the end, the French team snatched the victory and went on to beat their fellow countrymen, Perpignan, in the final. After the game we were bussed back to the airport and, unlike the thousands of other Munster supporters in Toulouse Airport, we were given VIP treatment and taken out to our 'private' jet for the return journey.

Unfortunately JetMagic only lasted a short time and went into liquidation in less than a year.

– 32 –

Back Down Under

With the Rugby World Cup, the Melbourne Cup and the Compromise Rules games all on at the same time in Australia 2003, Jerry Mackey and I decided we could not let a sports feast like that take place without our presence, so we headed off again.

We stopped in Singapore en route and were stunned by the heat and humidity – even walking was a chore – so when we heard you could do a zoo safari by night we jumped at the chance! It was fascinating seeing the animals in their habitat by night. The final piece of the tour trail included a bat house and it was amazing to see bats up close moving around and hanging upside down asleep.

I knew that my pal Mark Landers was in town so I texted him and we met up with him and his friends Johnny Irwin and the great Joe Deane. The lads were playing pool to the amazement of the locals. One of the locals put his money on the table to take on Joe. The guy was full of it, with all the moves, cigarette out the side of his mouth, chalking the cue, walking around like the world champion. Joe let the guy break and he never saw the table again as Joe demolished him. The showman left in disgust. I expect Joe would excel at anything he took on.

We left the Killeagh lads and made our way back to our hotel as we had an early flight to Perth in the morning. After a seven-hour flight we began to explore the beauty of Perth, a lovely, clean city. We found the Perth cricket ground and were fascinated by some of the signs: one said 'No Smoking in the Stadium', which was fair enough, but the next one was 'No Thongs Allowed'. We wondered who had the awful job of checking ladies underwear. We found out later that it meant flip-flop sandals.

We met the Irish compromise team who were staying at the beautiful five-star Hyatt Hotel. They were all in great form and really looking forward to the first game on the Friday in Perth Municipal Ground. It was a tough game and it took the Irish lads a while to get into it. The Aussies were handy winners.

A four-hour flight got us to Melbourne, where I was met by my niece, Jackie, one of Eamon's daughters. Like a lot of Irish youngsters Jackie was in Australia for a year trying to 'find' herself. We had booked a hotel on the outskirts of the fine city of Melbourne which was handy as the tram stopped about a hundred yards up the street. There was a huge Irish gathering in Melbourne as the rugby team was playing the Aussies, there was the second test of the compromise rules, plus the Melbourne Cup, all in the space of five days.

Another niece, Eimear Connery, was also 'finding' herself in Sydney and arrived to meet her favourite uncle with some friends from Waterford. Of course, Damien the Doc turned up, as did the photographer Donna McBride. We all met up and spent time together. Jackie was staying in a house with Ian Gardiner and his girlfriend, Caroline, from home, also on the same mission of locating themselves. One night Damien was meeting a few friends for a meal and invited Jerry and me along to the most expensive restaurant in Melbourne, where a steak cost $80. We had to live on bags of chips for the rest of our stay.

Our hotel was a short distance from Flemington racecourse so one day Jerry and I took the tram there for a look. There was a lot of security personnel but we walked around as if we were VIPs and no-one took any notice of us. We entered the VIP areas, all the stands and tent areas, and were never stopped. There are six different tracks in Flemington and we crossed each one without any attention. We then walked around the Melbourne Cup course and got a good feel for the place. So much for their security system.

On the Friday night it seemed like the whole of Ireland was in Melbourne for the compromise rules game. 60,000 fans turned up including Tara Spain, Gary's sister, and her friends Lenny and Lillian. There was a great atmosphere all around the Melbourne cricket ground where the match was taking place, but once again the Aussies were too powerful and ran out easy winners. This was the first time that a touring side had lost a series, but as usual we Paddies celebrated as if we had won.

On the Saturday night it was time to head to the Tel

Star Dome, where the rugby was taking place. Another huge Irish crowd, but not as big as the night before. It appears that Aussie rules is more popular than rugby in Australia. As the teams lined up before the game, the entire crowd stood up except Jerry and me for that terrible 'Ireland's Call'. Three men with deep Northern Ireland accents alongside us asked, 'why ye's not standing for our national anthem?' I said, 'When are they going to play it?' He passed some other smart remark but we stayed sitting. Then, out of respect, we got up for the Aussie national anthem and our three Northern brethren gave us a strange look.

The rugby match was not a great one from an Irish point of view as the team lost, but it was historical in another way in that it was the first time that a president of the GAA had attended a rugby match in an official capacity. My niece Jackie and her friends, who had no tickets, went to a nearby pub to watch the first half. Because of the no smoking policy in grounds in Australia, the gates have to be open to let people out for a smoke outside the stadium. There is a 'no pass out' system in operation, so anyone can walk in and watch the second half of an event, as Jackie and her friends did.

The gates into Flemington racecourse open at 7 a.m. on the day of the Melbourne Cup. This is the biggest sporting event in Australia and is held on the first Tuesday of November each year, an unofficial bank holiday. We had got our ground tickets before we went out to Australia. There was one Irish horse to take part in 2003 and that was the Willie Mullins-trained *Holy Orders*. He got great attention from the media, as he threw a few wobblies in front of the television cameras. We decided to back him out of patriotism, if nothing else.

The day of the races we were up early and headed by train to the racecourse on a very hot day. The first two people we met were our old friends from Youghal, Con Spillane and Ger Twomey. The crowd was huge, the official figure was 122,000 people. Everyone was lying or posing on the grass with their bottles of Champagne. We found a nice quiet corner behind the stands, where the bookies are located, and made this our base. The excitement mounted throughout the day. The first race was off at 10.30 a.m. with more every fifty minutes until the big one. The favourite was *Mumify* but he was withdrawn lame so the new favourite became *Mamoul* ridden by Frankie Dettori.

As the time approached for the race I thought we would see nothing at ground level so I went up to one of the stands. I spotted that the security guard was exhausted and was only glancing at the tickets so when I saw a crowd going past him with ease I decided I would chance putting my hand over the part of the ticket that said Ground Admission Only and got in. It is my opinion that all stewards, gardaí and security staff at big events are at their sharpest at the start of the day, but as the day wears on and the tiredness and boredom set in, they get less vigilant and it is easy enough to get past them. This happens from Pairc Uí Chaoimh, to Croke Park, to a World Cup final.

Once I was in the stand I told Jerry, Con and Ger what I had done and told them to do the same, which they did, so we had a great view of the race which was won by *Makybe Diva* at 8/1. We were so exhausted from walking, standing and trying to get through the crowds that the minute the Melbourne Cup was over we headed back to our hotel.

Our second visit to the land down under finished with my getting the flu, which made for a long journey home. In Melbourne Airport's departure lounge we saw the mural which is a great tribute to a great Irish man, Ronnie Delaney, celebrating his great gold medal at the Melbourne Olympics in 1956.

– 33 –

Kerr Takes the Reins

With Brian now in charge of the national senior team, despite the awful start to the campaign, everyone was full of optimism. Tony and I enthusiastically booked flights to the two away games in Georgia and Albania.

We headed off to Tbilisi from Cork via London. While in Heathrow, I pulled something in my back which affected my right hand. I got medical attention and tablets in the airport, which eased the pain, and was told to keep my hand in a sling. The only cloth I had which would make a sling was a tricolour, which had to do. On arrival in Tbilisi we had to fill out some forms to gain entry. I got through easily but after what seemed like an eternity Tony emerged from the immigration booth. It transpired that the lady could not get the hang of where Tony was born. He comes from a village in Limerick, called Hospital and she had to be convinced that it was a town, not a building.

I switched on my mobile and there was a message from Brian Kerr, seeing if we had arrived and telling us that he had tickets for us. A courtesy car, from Georgia Tourism, which Sonia our travel agent had booked for us when she heard about my injury, met us and took us to our hotel. But not before we went to the team hotel, where we received a big welcome from the management team. Enquiries were made about my hand and back, and Brian arranged for me to see the team doctor the following morning who put me through some severe tests and recommended that I keep the sling on and gave me some pain killers.

The day of the match Tony and I went to the stadium early and were inside the perimeter fence when some of the Irish media came along and tried to get in. The security man told them they would have to go the whole way round the compound. I had been talking to a policeman at the time they arrived and I got him to let the reporters in, so Tom Humphries and Emmet Malone were spared the long walk around the ground. Tom later that week wrote in his column in the *Irish Times*:

> Everywhere I go in the world for sport I notice something else. They have Jim Ryan and Tony O'Sullivan from Cork. Everywhere. We were floating along on Saturday night along the perimeter of the Lokomotiv Stadium looking for the entrance to the ground and there on the other side of the railings, inevitably, were Jim Ryan and Tony O'Sullivan from Cork. Soon they were pointing to us and explaining to the security blockheads that these guys were media, they were okay. Vouchsafed by Jim Ryan and Tony O'Sullivan from Cork we got in.
>
> Now this was a night when even Davy Keogh wasn't saying hello. I have no doubt when Amundsen made it to the South Pole the two figures he could see from hundreds of miles away turned out to be Jim and Tony just waiting around to shake his hand.

> Jim and Tony make their own way to these places. Youth games in Nigeria. Play-offs in Tehran. Qualifiers in Tbilisi. If they aren't there a FIFA rule kicks in about the game being invalid. Just in case, Brian Kerr texted them the other day to make sure they had tickets. I can't imagine the golf in Florida or the rugby in Lansdowne actually took place yesterday. Jim and Tony were here working out how to get to Tirana.
> Tom Humphries
> Locker Room, Monday, March 31, 2003.

The Georgians are big into wearing black leather, so the stadium was a sea of black with the odd patch of green. There was a very small Irish crowd, about a hundred or so in all, and we were all herded into one corner including the under-21 team who had played the night before. The match got Brian's term as manager off to a great start after the win in Scotland and now a 2–1 win away in the European qualifiers. But there was an uphill battle to qualify after the first two defeats to Russia and Switzerland.

After the game it became hostile as some of their supporters started throwing knives and blades at the Irish players, but it was brought under control by the thousands of police officers who attended the game. Tony and I headed to the safety of the under-21 bus and invited ourselves on board. This bus drove past any danger, even though a number of objects were thrown at the bus as we left the ground. The next morning we tried to get to Tirana, but to no avail, and we were told that there were no seats left on the flight, even though we heard afterwards that there was at least six seats empty. We saw off the teams and spent the day sightseeing around Tbilisi. Next morning we got a taxi to the airport, which was an experience in itself. The car would slow down while it made its way in and out of a huge pothole. There were lots of these craters. At home we really don't have potholes at all.

When we arrived in the airport, we were told that our flight to London was delayed twelve hours. We heard that when the plane was on its way to Georgia, the pilot got a threatened heart attack and they had to land in Abu Dhabi. The incoming flight was delayed four hours, and then the crew had to rest for eight hours.

While waiting at the airport we met a few interesting people. One guy worked on oil wells all round the Soviet Republic. It had taken him two days by car to get to Tbilisi for his flight to London, so another twelve hours wasn't going to worry him. Another chap had been in Tbilisi at the match with the company that put up the electronic advertising boards around the pitches. I then got talking to a man who was vice president of the Georgian Rugby Union, who told me that rugby was huge in Georgia and he hoped it would not be long before they would be able to compete in the A League. On the Sunday before, Georgia had played in the B Six Nations in Tbilisi and 60,000 had attended the game while only 19,000 had attended the soccer match.

We got into London late and missed our connection to Dublin, but Aer Lingus would not change our tickets to Cork. We eventually got into Dublin about 1 a.m., wrecked. After the disappointment of not getting to Tirana, we had

Myself and Brian Kerr

to be satisfied with watching the match against Albania on television. It was a great match with a nil-all draw, so with the two away games we had picked up four points and were kind of back on track again. These two matches were followed by the return matches against the same opposition in which Ireland beat both Albania and Georgia in Dublin. Then came the defining moment in the group when we failed to beat Russia in Dublin and could only achieve a 1–1 draw.

So now it was down to the final match in the group against Switzerland in Basle. We decided to fly from Kerry to Frankfurt Hahn, where we would pick up a car and drive down through Germany and onto Basle. Tony, Jessy and I were joined on the trip by an old friend from Japan, Vince. We headed down the motorway and stayed overnight in a quiet German town called Speyer, which is down the motorway from a place called Worms. When we arrived at the Swiss border, on the outskirts of Basle we had to pay a tax which allowed us to drive in Switzerland on all the motorways. It lasts for a year and little did we think that we would be back again within the year.

After a little difficulty we found our hotel, which was a lovely train ride to the city centre. Basle has a great tram and public transport system. When you book into a hotel you get vouchers which enable you to travel free on the trams. That evening we drove down the country to a town call Neuchatel where the under-21 team was playing. The manager of Neuchatel team is Don Givens, a former senior international and top scorer for many years. After his playing days in England, Don went to Switzerland and played with Neuchatel in the Swiss league. He got a great reception from the locals when he led out his team, who played out a nil-all draw. Gary Spain and his sister Tara arrived in Neuchatel by train and we all travelled back to Basle. At this stage the city was swarming with green clad people and there was a great buzz around the place. Damien Greene arrived, as did Mairead O'Callaghan, and many more friends. These trips are like reunions of the same people when you are away. You may never see them at home.

The match itself was a huge disappointment, as our expectations were so high, and we lost 2–0 after a very hard physical game.

– 34 –

The Olympics, Athens

When the announcement came through that the 2004 Olympics were to be held in Athens, I knew I had to go. As flights were difficult to get I came up with a plan and booked a package holiday to Corfu from where I could make my way to the mainland. Accommodation in Athens also proved elusive so one day I got on to Neil Prendeville on 96FM in Cork, and put out a plea for a spare room. I was introduced to one of the respondents, Mary Barrett, over the air the very next day.

Mary offered her daughter, Sinead's, apartment in Athens. As it happened, I knew the family very well as they lived on Richmond Hill in Cork and knew friends of mine. I left for Corfu like a lost sheep on my own and arrived at my apartment, which I was leaving again the next day. After a meal I met with some people from Northern Ireland and we got talking about the Olympics and the merits of trying to get gaelic football into the Olympics. Next day I left Corfu and arrived in Athens Airport about a half hour before Damien the Doc. We got a bus to the harbour where we met Sinead, who graciously agreed to put up the two of us for the next few days.

We had already chosen our tickets carefully: the rowing finals, as we expected Gearoid Towey and Sam Lynch to be in the final; the 20km walk for Gillian O'Sullivan; my cousin Jamie Costine in the 50k walk; and of course we were rooting for Andy Lee in the boxing and Sonia O'Sullivan in the 5,000 metres.

Unfortunately it all went pear-shaped: Gearoid and Sam lost the semi-final; Gillian O'Sullivan got injured and didn't take part; Jamie was involved in a horrific traffic accident in Greece a few days before I arrived; Andy Lee was beaten in his first fight; and Sonia ran her final race in the Olympics when she was lapped and finished last. She still got a standing ovation though as she made her way around the track alone which was a measure of her standing in world athletics. The whole stadium gave her the send-off she deserved – it was a great moment in sport.

I did a number of interviews for 96FM from Athens. One such interview was from the Olympic stadium, where it was so noisy I ended up in a toilet under the stand. It was the first time Neil Prendeville had spoken to anyone live from a lavatory.

On the Sunday morning, we headed out to the rowing finals in which an Irish 4s were taking part. We got up at 5 a.m. and by 8 a.m. the heat was close to unbearable. We met a lot of neighbours from Fermoy, including Paul Kavanagh, Richie Hogan, my old sergeant, and Gerry Towey, an older sergeant of mine from Mitchelstown.

I developed a nasty case of shingles and the soreness

increased with the heat. I was exhausted. I left Athens on the Wednesday after five days of poor results for the Irish and feeling quite unwell. I returned to Corfu and then to Cork via Dublin.

– 35 –

World Cup 2006

After the disappointment of not qualifying for Euro 2004 came a number of very attractive friendly fixtures for the senior team. The first in Dublin was a 3–0 win over Canada, followed by a group of three matches at home starting with a great nil-all draw against Brazil. On 31 March 2004, the day I retired, we won 2–1 over the Czech republic and went on to draw nil-all on an away trip to Poland. This was followed by a match in Dublin with Romania, a game in which Roy Keane made a return to the Irish team.

The trip to Poland was a lovely experience. The flight was early so we walked around Warsaw Airport where I saw a sign for the Marriott Hotel. I went over to investigate and met a woman called Anna who it turned out had learned her English when working in the Achill B&B on Western Road, Cork, while her boyfriend worked in the Eastern Tandoori Indian restaurant near the Opera House. The conversation got better as she knew of a former colleague of mine, Con Lucey, who owns another B&B on Western Road. She booked Tony, Jessy and me into the

Marriott Hotel. I asked her to join us for dinner later and she took us to a beautiful, traditional Polish restaurant and after dinner gave us a tour of Warsaw.

Before we left I had hired a car and picked it up at the airport. The countryside and country roads in Poland are similar to here and as we drove along the road to a town called Grudziadz for the under-21 game, it was like being at home. After the game we headed for Bydgoszez where the senior game was to be played the next day. After meeting some of the Irish media personnel, we booked into their hotel and got a fabulous room for the three of us for about €30 each.

The next day I was walking down a street in Bydgoszez when I met a friend, Enda McEvoy, the *Sunday Tribune* columnist. We were both in Irish jerseys and sat down for a chat. After a few minutes, a man approached us and said 'Conas tá tú?' 'Go maith agus tú féin?' we replied in unison. He told us he was Polish and that he had worked in the bar on the Cork–Swansea ferry and the lorry drivers had taught him bits of Irish. It was a lovely moment. The match was a drab nil-all draw, so we decided to head back to Warsaw, about a three-hour drive. On the way we stopped at a shop/chipper/pub in the middle of nowhere to get refreshments, and I noticed the guy behind the counter had a pen with the name Letterkenny on it. It transpired they had visited Donegal the previous year.

The campaign for the World Cup in Germany 2006 started with a 3–0 win over Cyprus in Dublin on 4 September. This was followed a week later with another trip to Basle in Switzerland for the away game against the Swiss. We flew our normal way from Kerry to Frankfurt Hahn in Germany, and drove south. On this occasion we had a top of the range brand new Vauxhall ten-seater van, what a babe to drive! We got most of the way before stopping and saw a sign for a town called Feilbeirg, where we got a hotel for about €30 each for the night. This is the place where the town clock rings every morning at 7 a.m. to awaken the townspeople. It was here also that I discovered that there is a 25c tax on glass bottles since the Second World War.

We left Feilbeirg and headed for the border in our silver *A-Team* style van. We paid the toll tax at the border and headed to our city centre hotel. It was there that while reversing into a space outside the hotel, I scraped our beautiful van on a bollard which I had not seen. Though the damage was small, it was sickening to have damaged such a beautiful vehicle. Fortunately the insurance covered the repairs. We checked into our hotel and some of us headed to Bern for the under-21 game where Cork City's Liam Kearney and Kevin Doyle were playing. The team lost that game.

The senior game was a sell-out and as we made our way to the stadium, we met an old friend, Joe Lynch, who was Irish ambassador in Nigeria when Tony and I were there in 1999, and is now the Irish ambassador in Switzerland. There was a great buzz in the stadium. Roy Keane played well and once again Shay Givens was brilliant. We were happy with the 1–1 draw. After the match we met

Brian Kerr who was also happy with the draw and so we all had a good night.

Next morning we headed back to Kahn in our now slightly scarred van and on the way stopped off at Hockenhein Ring, the formula one course. There we enjoyed the museum and saw some cars being tested. As we headed back to Kahn, we must have been caught on speed cameras as I later received a summons for speeding. They are still coming as I didn't pay the first one I got – it looked like a cheque and I only discovered my mistake when I went to the bank to cash it.

Back home in Cork, it was time to start packing again for Paris three weeks later on 8 October 2004. On our first day we took a cruise down the Seine, under the Eiffel Tower – a beautiful sight when lit up at night. The tour was going great until the boat broke down and we had to be towed to the quayside. We all changed over to another boat and continued our trip under the famous bridges of Paris.

We awoke on the Saturday morning to torrential rain and, horror of horrors, the mobile phone system had crashed perhaps due to the huge volume of Irish who descended on Paris for that weekend. The funny thing was that we all managed to meet one another, despite the lack of phones on which we had become too dependent. I found Paris to be expensive, at least where we drank. That first day a beer, tea for two and a hot chocolate cost me €26!

The game in the Parc de France was like a home game with up to 35,000 green-clad enthusiasts all round the stadium – a large number when you consider that Lansdowne Road can only accommodate 33,000. It was a super game with Shay Givens making some world-class saves, and John O'Shea missing an open goal. Our team stunned the French with their play and we were unlucky not to get a win; still, a nil-all draw was a good result. On the Sunday we travelled back to Cork and went straight to Pairc Uí Chaoimh for the county hurling semi-finals.

The following Wednesday it was off to Dublin for the home game against the Faroe Islands, a game in which Robbie Keane created a new scoring record for Ireland. The match was also memorable for a wonderful move by Damien Duff which resulted in him being brought down for a penalty. At the match I met some reporters from the Faroe Islands who filled us in on how to get there for the return leg.

There was a break in the championship campaign while the team played and beat both Croatia and Portugal in Dublin, so our next match was to be against Israel in Tel Aviv on 26 March 2005, which happened to be Easter Saturday.

The plan came together and it was early on 23 March 2005 that we gathered at Cork Airport for our flight to Prague; this was to be my fourth time in Prague in a year. When we arrived we got a taxi bus straight to Prague Castle to see the changing of the guard at midday, then we made our way to the Infant of Prague Church and onto the Astronomical Clock. As our flight to Tel Aviv was not until midnight, we booked two boxes at the Opera House for a performance of La Bohème. It was lucky that we had the boxes where no-one could see us slide onto the floor for a snooze, where it was more comfortable than the seats.

When the show was over we got the taxi bus back to the airport. We had been told that we would have a lot of trouble at Tel Aviv Airport and that it could take up to three hours to get through customs and police checks. When we arrived, we walked off the plane and straight through all the checks and were at the baggage area to collect our bags in no time. Except, of course, my bag did not arrive. Luckily enough I always take a shoulder bag with a change of essentials.

We went to the car rental area and picked up our ten-seater van to head to our hotel in Jerusalem, where we checked in at 8 a.m. They were very good in the hotel and let us into the rooms at that time so we could get some sleep. As it was Holy Thursday, it was a great time to be in Jerusalem, so we visited all the sites, such as the Knesset (house of parliament). From there we got two taxis, one driver an Israeli and the other one an Arab, who took us to Bethlehem, where we were introduced to their friends, the Palestinians, who took us on a tour of the area. This included the Church of the Assumption, Mount of Olives and the stable where Jesus was said to have been born. It was Holy Thursday and Good Friday but all the ceremonies were low key and respectful with very little commercial activity. We also saw the wall that the Israelis are building all around the country to cut off the Palestinians.

The following day I asked the Arab taximan to drive our van as it would be cheaper and easier than taking two taxis. He agreed and he took us to all the best sites, including the Garden of Gethsemane where he was able to jump the queue, no questions asked, and on to the Wailing Wall. The whole experience really brought the Gospel to life.

As some of us were going to Tel Aviv for the under-21 match on Good Friday, we left Jerusalem and headed to that game. The others followed later in a taxi, and we all met up at our hotel, where my bag had arrived.

A big crowd was gathering for the senior game and as we hung about the beach area of Tel Aviv, which is the city's centre, more and more of the green army arrived from all different parts.

As we were expecting to win, the match itself was very disappointing: we took the lead but later on let the home team get an equaliser. The following morning some of our party left to go home, but the five of us stayed on and headed off through the desert south towards Eilat which is the southernmost tip of Israel with its border with Egypt and the Red Sea. The five-hour journey was hot so we were lucky we had an air-conditioned van. The road was smooth, but it was fascinating to see the rolling desert on both sides with no sign of life. Along the way we stopped in tiny villages where we had teas and coffees and honey-covered sweet cakes.

Having arrived in Eilat, after a little confusion at our hotel which claimed not to have heard of us, despite a booking reference number, we got our room and settled in to this very quiet area.

The following morning I went for a dip in the Red Sea, which was lovely and warm, blue and not red. Some of our party tried to cross over to Egypt, but it was going to take a few hours to get through the red tape so that idea was aborted and instead we all chilled out by the swimming pool in the hotel. After two days in Eilat it was time to head north again, this time up the coast along by the Red Sea with Jordan on our right. It was on this road that we came to Masada located at the top of an isolated rock on the edge of the Judean desert and the Dead Sea valley. King Herod is said to have fled there in 40BC with his family and fortified it. Now in ruins, we got a feel for the way people protected themselves against the elements and invaders. We had to get a cable car up there, which had a spectacular view of the vast valley below.

As we moved on, we came across a sign for Lott's wife, who was turned into a pillar of salt, and we found her standing there looking down on the Dead Sea. I noted that she still doesn't look well and found it amazing that no-one knew her first name. You can make out the face from a carving high up, looking down over the Dead Sea.

We then called to the entrance to the Dead Sea which has a barrier and office where you pay for a visit, but it was closed so we headed off and went to Jericho. First of all we met an Israeli checkpoint and the guard told us he knew nothing about Jericho, despite the fact that they had occupied it up to the week before. We moved 200 yards down the road to the Palestinian checkpoint, where they also told us they knew nothing about Jericho but, like the

Israelis, were delighted to see us, with our tricolour flying out of the van.

We called to a magnificent building just outside Jericho which turned out to be the Intercontinental Hotel. We were surprised to find it was only €45 B&B. We had landed on our feet in a five-star hotel with four swimming pools – one for each of us and another for when we got bored of our own. Gambling is illegal in Israel but this hotel was built on Palestinian land so now all the Israelis come there and gamble away to their hearts' content. The manager told us that during the busy season he would take in $1 million a day. This was now off-season and we were the only people staying in the hotel but they kept all the staff on for us.

We went for a meal in a restaurant in Jericho, where a full meal and drinks came to less than €12 each. The next day we visited the Dead Sea, which was not dead, but very much alive and grey in colour, and where I had the most amazing experience. Though I cannot swim or float, in the Dead Sea I managed both which, for me, was an amazing experience. I have always been afraid of drowning but I felt perfectly confident here. We came out of the Dead Sea, which is full of salt, and then covered ourselves in mud in a mud bath. I turned to a man next to us who had an Irish accent; he turned out to be the Irish ambassador to Israel.

After this experience we headed to Tel Aviv again. Each time we passed through the checkpoints we got a great reception from the Palestinians and Israelis in turn. They

Above: visiting Lott's wife; below: visiting Arafat's grave

were happy to see the French taking on the home team. We went to the match where we enjoyed a great atmosphere among the Israeli supporters, particularly when the Israelis got a late goal to get another draw. The few days we spent in Jericho were great as some of the party went to the Sea of Galilee and Nazareth, while we all went to the Walls of Jericho and took the cable car, again, up to a monastery which was built into the mountain where Our Lord is said to have fasted for forty days and nights.

Another highlight of our stay was a trip to Ramala in the West Bank, where we found the Palestinian compound where Yasser Arafat lived and where he is now buried. We arrived in an Israeli van, so the Palestinians were suspicious of us until we explained that it was a hired van and we were Irish. The change of attitude towards us was amazing and the welcome we got was outstanding. We were brought to the tomb where Arafat is buried and were allowed to take photographs and we added to the flags on the grave by leaving a tricolour on it. It was brilliant to see all the places we had learned about in our religion classes in primary school.

We had hardly arrived home before we started planning our trip for the return match against the Faroe Islands. When we first heard we were drawn against them in our group, we knew it was going to be a hard job to get there. The Faroes are a group of islands in the Norwegian Sea, halfway between Scotland and Iceland. Gary Spain and I looked at all the different ways of getting there and even went as far as enquiring about chartering a plane ourselves. This turned out to be a non-runner, due to financial restraints; all the chartering companies were looking for about €20,000 for a twenty-seater jet. I also spoke to Ryanair to see if they would do a charter, but was told that the airport in Tórshavn was too small to land one of their planes. We eventually came across a travel agent in Dublin who had a tie-up with a supporters club and was organising a two-day trip for around €750. They also had day trips going and so we opted for that.

It was with great expectation that Tony, Jessy, Jerry and I headed to Dublin on Tuesday, 7 June 2005, for our trip to the Faroe Islands. We had been in Dublin the Saturday before at the return leg with Israel in which we raced into a 2–0 lead, but somehow the Israelis struck late again and snatched a 2–2 draw, which turned out to be very costly in the competition. We had dropped four points to Israel, but at least we were not the only ones in our group: the French and Swiss had similar fates.

We arrived at Dublin Airport very early on 7 June and checked in. Everything appeared normal as we went through customs and passport control. The first indication that anything was wrong was when I received a text from Damien, who was on a day trip also, but had left Dublin Airport earlier than us. They were heading towards Norway as there was fog on the Faroes and the plane could not land there. We waited and waited and waited, rumour following all the rumours about what was happening. Damien texted again that their pilot said he was going to try again as he wanted to go to the match too.

There was no-one from our travel agents to tell us what was happening. We were in contact with some of the management who told us that the fog was so bad that the match was in danger of not going ahead. Apparently there had not been weather like it in the Faroes for twenty years. Damien texted again to tell us that the pilot was going to wait awhile before he tried again. All the time we were under the impression that our planes were on the ground in Dublin Airport. It transpired that they had never left the Faroes, so the deadline was set at 1.30 and if they did not leave the Faroes by that time there was no way they would get to Dublin and back again in time for the match.

As 1.30 approached it became obvious we would not get there. While we waited for the eight hours for our plane, several attempts were made by staff at the airport to move us from a tea-drinking area to the bar as one or two of the lads had a bottle of wine and it is apparently a mortal sin to drink a glass of wine in a tea-drinking area. It was ironic that as we sat nice and quietly having quiet conversations we were the ones who were asked to move into a very noisy and now hostile bar of Irish supporters.

At 1.30 p.m. the announcement was made that the flight to the Faroes was cancelled so we had to go in search of our bags which had already been checked through. We found them and headed back to the car for the journey back to Cork where we saw the lads having a very convincing 2–0 win against the home side.

I always take out travel insurance, a yearly one is the best, but after the run around I got from the travel agent and then the insurance company, I wondered what I had insurance for at all. They all said it was an Act of God, but my argument is that so is everything that delays a plane – fog, snow, storms, defects, bombs. The travel agent said they were not responsible as the plane never left the Faroes. The insurance company said they were not responsible; the Act of God argument, that deity has a lot to answer for. I was down €760. Eventually, after a year of hassling and appealing, I got some €500 back.

The next match was a friendly against Italy in Dublin in August 2005, in which we lost 2–1, and so we were into the final run towards Germany 2006. The first up was the home game against France, which was going quite well until a certain Mr Thierry Henry decided that he was going to upscuttle the Irish party by getting a gem of a goal. And so it was now down to the last two games in the group which we needed to win. First up was the away trip to Cyprus. We really went the scenic route to get to Larnaca and back, through Gatwick, with a bus to Heathrow from where we flew to Prague and onto Larnaca after a quick tour around the city for those who hadn't already seen the sights. The Irish media had started on Brian Kerr even before this game. I was trying to visualise the GAA press having a go off John Allen or Mick O'Dwyer on the week before an All-Ireland final. Here were the two most important matches that Ireland was going to play in a while, and some of the Irish media, some would think instigated by the FAI officials, were having a right go at Brian and trying to undermine his managerial ability. I thought this was very unfair, but then maybe I am biased as I think he was a good manager. In any case that was not the time to undermine the spirit of the team in a trial by media.

It obviously had the desired effect as the team played badly and was lucky to get out with a 1–0 win in front of a crowd of 11,000, of which 10,000 were Irish. We stayed at the same hotel we had stayed in before which was about a mile from the airport. We hired a car to travel around the island and this time including a visit to Northern Cyprus, which is occupied by Turkey. We travelled back straight after the game because when I booked the trip I had envisaged my beloved Hill would be in the county final; that did not materialise. We got back to Cork on the Sunday and got ourselves ready for the winner-takes-all match the following Wednesday in Dublin against Switzerland.

This was to be Ireland's 416th international and it ended in a nil-all draw, which was not enough for Ireland to get into the play-off, not to mind top the group. The dream of Germany 2006 was over and they all started on Brian. In no time he was sacked, unfairly I feel. As far as I was concerned it was trial by media and he wasn't flavour of the month. The Irish managerial career of Brian Kerr ended and in came Steve Staunton.

2005 had not been a great year for Irish soccer but it was a historic one for Cork sport. Tony and I had started travelling to Cork City's European games in 2004, when we travelled by car to Nijmegen in Holland. As 2005 progressed we also went to Stockholm followed by another few days in Prague where a huge Cork crowd converged

Myself, Denis Sheehan, Jerome Buttimer, Michael O'Riordain, John O'Regan and Dan Kearney after Watergrasshill had won the Cork intermediate hurling championship in 2004

on Charles Bridge and the other sites of the city. Cork City went on to win the league in a great end of season game against Derry City, which Cork had to win. The win had been well deserved after many years of trying, and it was great coming on the back of Blue Demon's winning the National League in basketball. The Cork camogie team regained the O'Duffy Cup, Cork hurlers retained the McCarthy Cup, and then a great Cork ladies football team – captained by Juliet Murphy and trained by my big brother, Eamon – took the National League title for the first time and on 2 October won the All-Ireland for the first time.

– 36 –

2006, Another Busy Year

The summer of 2006 was a busy one for me as, not alone was I involved with the team in Watergrasshill, but I also had to go and see Cork in their quest for the three-in-a-row hurling All-Ireland. On top of this was the Hockey World Cup, European Under-19 Soccer Cup and the 2006 World Cup in Germany.

My niece, Fiona, was playing for Ireland in the World Cup hockey qualifiers in Rome and so Tony and I headed to the Eternal City. We were joined by Mary and Kathleen a few days later.

The first night we went to see Ireland playing New Zealand and the rain was so severe that the pitch flooded and the first match had to be abandoned. These pitches are artificial and the drainage could not take the water. I have never seen rain like it, there was more rain in one hour than we would get in a year. The next morning the end of the first game and the whole of the Irish game were played in scorching sunshine, quite a contrast.

The thing about hockey tournaments is that the teams play every day which, in the heat and humidity of Rome, is severe on Irish players, who are amateurs. At this tournament the Irish played eight games in nine days in which it was great to see Fiona get her fiftieth Irish cap – a very proud moment. She has now been joined by her younger sister, Áine, who won her first senior cap against South Africa in January 2007 and played with her. For the record, the Irish girls did not qualify for the finals in Madrid in September 2006.

While in Rome we took in some of the sights, such as the Coliseum and the Vatican, even though the pope wasn't in. We also attended a reception hosted by Frank Cogan, the Irish ambassador to Italy, at the embassy and I had a long chat with him about Iran as he had been the ambassador in Tehran when I visited that country. We learned to be careful of taxi drivers in Rome who, if they think you don't know where you are going, will take you for a real ride. Two exceptions to this were the guys who took us to the Olympic Stadium where Lazio were playing a league match, and who brought us back to the airport via the countryside and only charged us €20 for the same trip that cost us €45 the first time.

Tony and I arrived at the Olympic Stadium about one and a half hours before kick off and went to buy match tickets. We were told we had to go to the Lazio club shop, which was about a half mile away, where we found a long queue. At one stage I went to the top of the queue to see what was the matter and found that they were only allowing four people in at a time, and if one of them wanted to buy anything from the shop, no one else got in until that person was finished browsing. The result was that kick-off time came and went and we were still way off the top of the queue. We are nothing but resilient though and stuck it out, eventually getting our tickets and arriving at the ground just coming up to half time. We had missed nothing. As we sat in the half-empty stadium, watching as these wimps fell over at any touch or no touch, I was reminded that if any of them came up against the great Mick Lyons of Meath or the late Humphrey Kelleher of Cork they would never play again, never mind get up off the ground. The heat got to us, along with the lack of excitement of the game and Tony and I nodded off to sleep with boredom, while Lazio got a late goal to win the match.

After the excitement of Rome it was time to head back home for a week to tidy up a few loose ends, before we headed off again, this time to Slovakia to see the Irish under-19 soccer team compete in the elite section of the European qualifiers against Slovakia, Georgia and Turkey with only one to qualify for the finals in Poland.

When we arrived in Bratislava, we picked up our car and headed up the country to the first town where the Irish team was playing. On our way along the highway, we saw a sign for Senec, the second town that we were playing, so we did a little detour, booked two beds for the Saturday night, and then headed to Nitra. The games were very disappointing, with three defeats in the three games.

On the Saturday we drove into Bratislava and found an Irish pub that was showing the Heineken Cup final between Munster and Biarritz, which proved to be a historical day for Munster and, I must admit, even though I'm not a big rugby fan, I shed a tear at the final whistle.

Our hotel in Senec was lovely in a beautiful setting on a lake, and it cost us just €60 for two per night with free access to a wonderful water complex across the road. This was a great facility: there was a small cover charge and in exchange you got indoor, outdoor and kiddies pools, hot tubs, jacuzzis, steam room, and a terrific power water jet system for back ailments. There should be one of these in every town in Ireland, but as soon as any project like this is mentioned the constant objectors come out of the woodwork and the price of construction soars. Our town councillors should pay a visit to see how it works.

As usual when we have a car with us on these visits we drive deep into the countryside and enjoy the hospitality of the locals in the villages. We really enjoy these visits as you meet the real people. One thing we noticed was the lack of cattle and sheep out in the fields that had stuck us also in Poland. We heard it had something to do with the Russian invasion when all the livestock was taken and not replaced. I noticed the same in the Czech Republic the week after, where I attended the wedding of my cousin, Michelle, and David, along with half of Watergrasshill. The wedding ceremony was in a castle about an hour's drive out the country. All the guests were bussed out there and Michelle was also in the convoy but in a lovely limousine. The buses took a wrong turning and the limo went the right way which, as the groom and his best man were in the second bus behind us, meant it must have been the first wedding in history that the bride was the first to arrive for the ceremony. The bride and groom were greeted to applause from the many tourists at the castle and the reception was held in a spectacular medieval banqueting hall. The usual places in Prague were visited again for the umpteenth time – the Castle, Charles Bridge, Infant of Prague, various churches and, of course, the Astronomical Clock.

The following week we started an assault on the World Cup in Germany. Months previously the attack had been launched with the booking of flights from Kerry Airport to Frankfurt Hahn and the booking of a car there for the purpose of going between venues. As our time was limited, we were going to go to matches in Frankfurt, Leipzig, and Munich or Stuttgart. I applied for tickets and received two for the France–Switzerland game in Stuttgart. There were four of us and I reckoned it would be difficult to get two more, so I gave these two to a friend, Karl Spain, who was going to this game anyway.

We picked up the car at Hahn and headed to Frankfurt to settle into our hotel. We then made our way into the city centre to try and get some tickets for the Togo–South Korea game, one we assumed would not be a sell-out. As we walked along I spotted this man with a badge who looked very official, and asked him was he with the Togo FA. I asked him if he had any tickets, and at first he said he hadn't but then he changed his mind and told us to be at the team hotel the following morning at 9 a.m. when he would have the only tickets left which would cost €120 each. We agreed to buy them, thinking they would

On the throne in Prague

be great tickets. We were at the hotel at 8.15 and eventually two guys arrived with the tickets. We asked for Paul Lombe, who was the man we had met, but they said they owned the tickets. We were handed the tickets, which were priced at €35 each, and I protested about the excessive price we were being charged. Still, I bit the bullet and handed over €480. I then asked if they would swap a Togo jersey for an Irish one. They agreed but wanted €25 each as well. Needless to say, we were not that stupid and they got the message loud and clear.

We headed out to the grounds early and we could sense a great buzz as we approached. The tickets we got were three together and one in the row in front. I gave Tony, Gerry and Eric the three together and said I would sit in the row on my own. The four of us lined up to be searched and the water bottles were taken from us; I often wonder about this as they allow flagpoles and flares. It doesn't make sense to me.

The three lads got in, but when my ticket was put in the turnstile it would not open it, showing up as a fault. I was taken to a ticket-office where I explained my case. I was told that the ticket had an incorrect number and that I would have to wait until just before kick off when I would get in if no-one came with the original. I waited in the fierce heat until half an hour before kick-off when I returned to the office to be told that the ticket had been cancelled and a new ticket reissued to someone else. Meanwhile, Jerry texted me that there were a huge amount of empty seats around them.

As luck would have it, I met my two tickets sellers who pretended they had never seen me before. However, I annoyed them so much that they told me the Big Chief would sort me out; Big Chief was an ordinary guy who was obviously the boss of this scam. He did his best to confuse the issue, talking a lot but giving me no information or solution to my problem of getting into the stadium; the two boys disappeared and I was left outside just at kick-off. The cops were of no help as they just referred me to an office too far away to bother. I returned to our hotel to watch it on television but unfortunately the match was not shown on German stations.

We decided not to go to another game as I had miscalculated the distances between cities in Germany and so, having spent the day in Frankfurt with Gary Spain, we headed back to Frankfurt Hahn where we got a reasonably apartment for the night and a good dinner.

When the draws for Euro 2008, to be played in Austria and Switzerland, were made, Ireland was in the same group as Germany, the Czech Republic, Slovakia, Wales and San Marino. The first match in the group was against Germany on Saturday, 2 September 2006, at 9.45 p.m. local time. Even as early as February 2006 I knew this was going to present a problem: I had no doubt that Cork senior hurlers would be in the All-Ireland final on 3 September and there was no way I was going to miss either match, so we got working on a plan.

On the Friday I drove to Dublin with Tony and Eric McNulty, Tony's nephew. We flew to Stansted, where we were joined by Damian Green, his father, George, Mairead O'Callaghan and Eileen Martin. We all waited a number of hours and headed off for Stuttgart in a new airline to us, German Wings, arriving at midnight. We got a taxi to the five-star Meridian hotel which we had booked at a reasonable rate before anyone had copped that the match would be held in Stuttgart. Gary Spain and his sister, Tara, joined us at the hotel which also happened to be where the German team was staying. We were now hobnobbing with the best in the world.

The next day there was a great atmosphere in the city centre as all the Irish from all over Europe arrived and created a massive party. There was a huge food fair and we sampled the culinary delights of Germany. I was the very proud Corkman as I wore my red t-shirt which said 'Irish by birth, Cork by the Grace of God'. After the match, which Ireland lost narrowly 1–0, we returned to the hotel and met most of the German players who turned out to be very friendly.

It was early to bed from me (1 a.m.) as were leaving three hours later to get to the airport for a 6 a.m. flight back to Stansted and onward to Dublin, arriving there at 1.30 p.m. Then the search of the vast Dublin Airport carpark for the car and the journey to Dublin city and Croke Park for Cork's day of destiny and our bid for the elusive three-in-a-row. Unfortunately it was not to be and we fell to a Kilkenny team on a day that they were slightly superior.

But what a great time all of us rebels have had following this great team and yes, there is more to come. I have to thank Jimmy Barry Murphy, Donie O'Grady, John Allen and their background staff for all the effort they have put into giving us such enjoyment over the years.

A three-in-a-row which was achieved in 2006 was that by St Lachtains camogie team from Freshford, Co. Kilkenny, in which my nieces Fiona, Eimear, Sinead and Áine Connery, all played their part in winning the All-Ireland Senior Club Camogie Championships in 2004, 2005 and 2006.

It was also great to witness the Cork camogie team win the O'Duffy cup for the second year on the trot as did the Juliet Murphy-captained and Eamon Ryan-trained Cork ladies football team who retained both the league and the championship after one of the better football games, men or women, of the year, against a very determined Armagh fifteen.

The next soccer match was the away game against Cyprus. I was not able to book a flight as my beloved Hill team was still in the championship and there was a possibility they could be playing that weekend. By the time I knew I could go to Cyprus the travel agents had lost the run of themselves and wanted anything up to €1,000 for a week in Cyprus in October, despite the fact that the week before and the week after you could have gone to Cyprus for €190. I love going abroad but I don't like travel agents taking advantage so I decided not to go. In any case I had been there twice already. Just as well, as it turned out to be one of the worst nights in soccer history with Cyprus beating Ireland 5–2. What a disgrace! However, the following Wednesday night in Lansdowne Road, the team surprised everyone to hold the crack Czech team to a 1–1

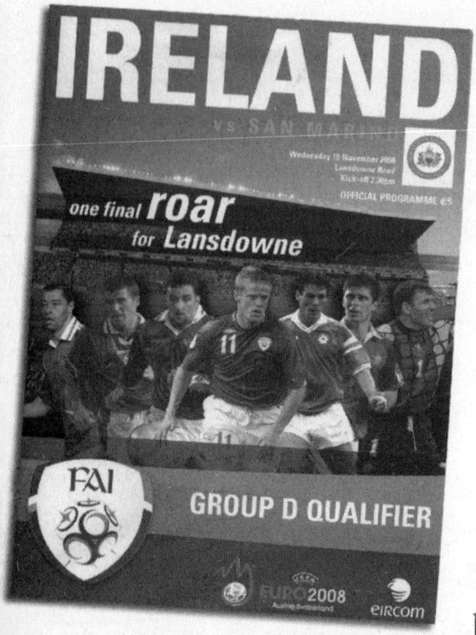

draw and all of a sudden the talk was that we were back on track again.

At the 2006 GAA congress in Croke Park, a very brave and historical decision was made to let the so-called 'foreign games' (soccer and rugby) be played in Croke Park as Lansdowne Road was to be knocked and rebuilt. So the honour of playing the last soccer match in the old Lansdowne Road pitch fell to Ireland and San Marino on 15 November 2006 with Ireland winning 5–0.

It was a big decision for the GAA to make, and as I write it is with great expectation that I look forward to the world seeing what an amazing stadium this amateur organisation has built.

Epilogue

I go to over 500 sporting events every year and would often go to four or five matches a day; my record was 19 over a long weekend. Sport and travel, I have found, are great ways of making friends and seeing the world at the same time. We Irish, being so good at so many sports, over the last few decades have had a great incentive to travel to countries we otherwise might never have bothered with. I have benefited from the success of Irish teams and individual sportspeople and have been privileged to have been present at their triumphs. This book is my humble tribute to them.

My thanks to the following who have accompanied me on my travels at different stages around the world:

Tony O'Sullivan, Jerry Mackey, Jerry O'Dwyer, Denis Murphy, Pat Higgins, John (Jessy) James, Catherine Ryan, Brendan Ryan, Gary Spain, Tara Spain, Damien (the Doc) Green, Mairead O'Callaghan, Eileen Martin, Eric McNulty, Yvonne McNulty, Jim (Jimmy Doc) Doherty, Catherine Connery, Mary Murphy, Mick O'Connor, Rose O'Connor, Tony Fitzgerald, Vince Cummins, Mick Hanley, Eddie McGough, John Riordan, Maureen Cotter, George Green, Mary Fitzgerald, Aileen Lane, Enda O'Brien, Liz Morrow, James Barry, Jack Joyce, Charlie Maher and the Tralee gang of Michael (Fox) O'Connor, John Magnier, Ger O'Gorman, Frank O'Connor and Jeremiah (La La) Fitzgerald.

To my wonderful travel agents, Sonia Blakeman, Caroline Jeffery, Mary O'Sullivan, Louise O'Riordan and others who helped me arrange the trips to some of the following: Northern Ireland, Scotland, Wales, England, Norway, Sweden, Denmark, Portugal, Spain, France, Belgium, Holland, Germany, Switzerland, Poland, Liechtenstein, Czech Republic, Slovakia, Italy, Austria, Sicily, Hungary, Yugoslavia, Croatia, Macedonia, Greece, Turkey, Romania, Bulgaria, Estonia, Latvia, Lithuania, Russia, Georgia, Azerbaijan, Iran, Belarus, Cyprus, Israel, Nigeria, Corfu, Japan, Korea, Singapore, Australia, USA and the Bahamas.

And to St Paul's Garda Credit Union who helped me out along the way.